Love in
Later Life

Also by the same author and published by Peter Owen
Hans Eysenck: The Man and His Work
Hypnosis: Its Nature and Therapeutic Uses
Pain and Its Conquest

H. B. GIBSON

Love in Later Life

PETER OWEN

LONDON & CHESTER SPRINGS

PETER OWEN PUBLISHERS
73 Kenway Road, London SW5 0RE
Peter Owen books are distributed in the USA by Dufour Editions Inc.,
Chester Springs, PA19425-0007

First published in Great Britain in 1997
© H. B. Gibson 1997
A catalogue record for this book is available from the British Library

ISBN 0 7206 1026 5

Printed in Great Britain by Biddles of Guildford and King's Lynn

Acknowledgements

In writing this book I am indebted to a large number of authors and have quoted quite liberally from their works. The principal books I have drawn from are listed among those cited at the end of the book as further reading. In writing about love I have scanned literature from the time of Plato onwards and given due weight to poets as well as those who have done painstaking surveys in this modern age.

My chief indebtedness is, of course, to the men and women who have been so kind as to send me the autobiographical accounts of their own experiences of forming new relationships in later life which are presented in Part 2 of this book. Without such accounts I would merely be writing about the topic as it has been in the past, without taking into consideration the great changes that have taken place in the past half-century that have radically altered our perception of ageing and the part love plays in the lives of older people.

In writing the book I have been greatly helped by the excellent advice and encouragement of Carol Graham, with whom I have been in constant discussion regarding both the contents and style.

Contents

Introduction   7

PART 1

1 What is love?   17
2 Late love in literature   38
3 Popular media images   57
4 New partnerships   73
5 Four late marriages   91
6 Staying together   124

PART 2

Cecily: 'Just a beginner'   141
Gertrude: 'His children were hostile'   149
Harriet: 'Marie and I would be lost without each other'   153
Susie: 'Friends warned me about the age gap'   158
Monica: 'A friendship between opposites'   163
Roger: 'The garden gets somewhat neglected'   171
Tina: 'I still love him dearly'   175
Tom: 'The man with two front doors'   190
Vera: 'My love is not returned, but I am content'   199
Charlie: 'Few would guess Bill will be eighty this summer'   201

Notes   207
Further reading   214

Introduction

This book is directed mainly to older people, but it will be of interest to everyone. Its subject is of perennial interest: love. We all experience love at some times in our lives, although love comes in many different forms. We are constantly reading about it, hearing about it on the radio, seeing it depicted on television. It is very much a part of our daily lives.

The writing of this book arose out of my widespread professional and social contacts with people in later life. I was producing a textbook on the emotional and sexual lives of older people, which was mainly aimed at social workers, doctors and other professionals,[1] and it occurred to me that there was a need for something on the theme directed to the reading public and that we should pay attention to older men and women speaking for themselves. From a variety of different sources I gathered autobiographical accounts by people who had formed new love relationships over the age of sixty, and I found most of them absolutely fascinating. All I required was that my contributors wrote simply and frankly, on the understanding that their identity would not be revealed. I was amazed and delighted at the variety of their experiences of love, some happy, some sad, some showing new insights into how we behave in later life and some engagingly comic. I have reproduced their accounts in Part 2, with very little alteration other than in minor changes of personal details to preserve the anonymity of the writers.

This book is unique, I think, and it would not have been possible to gather these frank autobiographical accounts a few years ago. That so many people have been willing to write of their intimate experiences is due to the changed and changing status of older people today. Until comparatively recently it was generally believed that men and women in later life had no sexual feelings or interest, and on the rare occasions on which elderly people remarried it was entirely for economic and social reasons. Indeed, it was regarded as indecent if older people showed the same erotic interests that are normally taken for granted in the young. In the famous Kinsey studies of the sexual lives of men and women that hit the headlines in the 1950s, although they interviewed hundreds of people in all walks of life they did not bother to interview more than a few individuals over the age of sixty because they took it for granted that people in this age group would have no interest in sex.[2] If they had done so forty years ago it is doubtful if they would have obtained truthful answers, because in those days such were the social pressures of the times that elderly people would have been ashamed to admit the reality of their sexual interests and practices.

Now things are very different. Older people have begun to rebel against the demeaning and frequently inaccurate stereotypes of 'the old' that have been handed down to us from our ancestors. No longer are elderly people expected to wear sombre clothing and to retire from active life. They are beginning to expect proper respect and will not tolerate being addressed as 'Dad' or 'Gran' by patronizing young officials. They wear clothes they find attractive and expect to adopt a lifestyle that is not noticeably different from that of people perhaps several decades younger than themselves. After a lifetime of work they are less willing to regard themselves as useless old things and to be grateful if their families exploit them as dogsbodies to look after the grandchildren on demand.

'Respectable' people no longer feel bound to show disapproval of elderly people who live together without being married or take lovers as do the young. In discussing bereavement in later life Wendy and Sally Greengross wrote in their important book *Living, Loving and Ageing,* 'The pain of this overwhelming loss is often made worse, because the surviving partner quite unexpectedly finds that he or she still has sexual feelings that demand satisfaction. Some of the need may be for touching, comfort and caring, but some people still have strong physical sexual desires.'[3]

Such a frank admission of the needs of elderly bereaved people would not have appeared in print many years earlier, although the facts have long been recognized but not discussed openly. To illustrate its point the book includes a cartoon of a notice-board in an old people's home inviting residents to volunteer for a range of activities: knitting, recipe swaps, bingo, pottery and 'Kama Sutra'. It is the last that has attracted by far the most numerous ticks, and an old lady is shown adding hers.

The fact is that, apart for the many old people struggling to live on inadequate pensions, many others of the same age have money to spend and, in contrast to previous generations, they do not feel impelled to live penuriously and hoard their money for the benefit of their inheritors. The spending power of a section of the older population has led to the publication of glossy magazines such as *Saga, Good Times, Active Life* and *Choice,* all of which are directed at an older readership and which advertise goods and services likely to appeal to such people. Some aspects of this commercialism may be regrettable, but this trend has helped to enhance the status of the elderly in modern society.

Not only have public attitudes changed to the extent that older couples who are not married can live together or share a hotel bedroom and no one raises any objection, but the alternative lifestyle of homosexual people is now tolerated. Among the autobiographical accounts of new love relationships being formed in later life, there is the description given by Harriet of how she fell in love with another woman when in her sixties and formed a very stable and happy lesbian partnership with her. Harriet had been married and had brought up children when younger but had drifted apart from her husband. It seems probable that such same-sex relationships between older women will become more common in future, because there is a growing numerical imbalance between the sexes as age advances. By the age of seventy-five there are nearly twice as many women as men left alive, so it would not be possible for more than a minority to form partnerships with men. I see that fine old feminist campaigner Betty Friedan in her book *The Fountain of Age* advocates polygamy in later life, one man being 'husband' to several women.[4] I think that this would be beyond the capacity of most elderly men!

Among the autobiographical accounts there is also that of Charlie, who formed a gay relationship with another man in his own age group after the age of sixty. Such new partnerships between older men are probably less common than those between women for the reason given above: that there are many more unattached women in later life. I think it is a mistake to regard the sexual orientation of men or women as being irrevocably fixed as heterosexual or otherwise except in a small minority of cases. It is probably the case that circumstances determine the direction of eroticism and love in many cases.

In Chapter 1 the nature of love is discussed. People mean different things by 'love'. In Part 2 Monica wonders whether the long-term sexual partnership she has formed with her man friend can truly be referred to as love. She writes, 'Love implies something of a romantic passion of the sort that we rarely feel in later years', but Vera does not agree with this view. She is quite certain that in her seventies she has 'fallen in love' and that the idyllic condition persists.

As many of our attitudes towards different forms of human behaviour are conditioned by the books we have read, and the attitudes of others around us who likewise are influenced by literature, Chapter 2 examines how love in older life has been depicted by writers throughout the ages. It is evident that throughout the centuries writers have tended to mock older people who show interest in sex, and this is part of the Western Christian tradition. It is only comparatively recently that the theme of love in later life is treated sympathetically in literature. This book also examines other cultures in which the theme is treated more sympathetically than in the West.

As in literature, so in the media love in old age has had a history of denial, neglect and derision, and this extends to popular humour where a cruel ageism depicts older people either dismissively or as a subject of mirth. This and related matters are discussed in Chapter 3. The term 'ageism,' which is often compared with 'racism' and 'sexism' to indicate a special sort of prejudice, was not coined until 1969, but it has now found a place in popular journalism. The world of advertising still exploits the presumed horrors of old age; women are constantly exhorted to buy expensive face creams 'guaranteed' to stave off the arrival of 'premature' wrinkles and hence preserve their sexual attractiveness. Another aspect of the exploitation of the ambivalence of society to the sexuality of the elderly is expressed in grossly offensive depictions of old people on humorous birthday cards.

Chapter 3 also relates the very recent history of love in later life as represented on television and radio. About twenty years ago the presence of older characters on television shows was rare. When they did appear it was either in the role of old dears mouthing platitudes or as figures of fun acting as foils for the more significant young characters. Depiction of the sexuality of the elderly was taboo. Nowadays the romantic and sexual affairs of older people feature regularly, and it is interesting to study

why this change has come about. It is illustrative of the changing position of the elderly in our society, who represent, after all,
an increasingly large proportion of the population.

In Chapter 4 I consider some objections to older people forming new love relationships. What are the practical consequences
of such relationships? How do the families of elderly lovers
react? What do doctors, social workers and those who run residential homes feel about their elderly clients having erotic experiences and aspirations? These questions need airing, for in some
circumstances it may be argued that we should damp down
rather than encourage the fires that provoke powerful emotions.

Many writers and social agencies are proclaiming that a new
age has arrived: an age in which older people are taking the
quite unprecedented step of claiming a liberty for themselves
that has not existed before, the liberty to love in whatever way
suits them. But this is not quite true; in previous ages, even in
the repressive Victorian era, those who were rich and powerful
enough have always flouted the age-bound conventions concerning sex and got away with it. Four cases of well-known people who formed new relationships in their later years are
described in Chapter 5. These may be compared with some of
the autobiographical accounts given in Part 2. What is new is
that these days quite ordinary older people can act in a way that
was previously possible only for those in the upper echelons of
society; moreover, whereas in former times it was almost wholly
the prerogative of men to form new love relationships in later
life, now it is principally women who do this, partly owing to the
advance of feminism and partly because the female sex is now in
a great majority in the later years.

Chapter 6 deals with the general question of love in later life
as it concerns couples in long-standing marital relationships.
The changes in social mores that have affected the relationships
of the young and middle-aged are now manifest in the marriages

of older people. The factors that make for their staying together 'till death do us part', as they did when divorce was a rarer occurrence, are examined in this chapter. Examples from a number of marriages are cited to reveal some surprising facts about the long-term relationships of older people in the modern world.

The autobiographical accounts given by contributors in Part 2 all concern new relationships that have been formed when one or both partners were over the age of sixty and illustrate a wide variety of experience.

Part 1

CHAPTER 1

What is love?

It may be thought that an inquiry into the nature of love would not be very appropriate for a book concerned with later life. In youth we are concerned with discovering the meaning of love in our first tentative explorations of sexuality and then, a little later, with finding a mate. In middle age we may explore the stormy seas of love, seas in which so many founder upon the rocks. This book is perhaps unique in showing that as long as we live and aspire to a meaningful and fulfilled life we are never free from the problems and the joys of love. The novelist Isaac Bashevis Singer writes, 'The love of the old and middle-aged is a theme that is recurring more and more in my works of fiction. Literature has neglected the old and their emotions. The novelists never told us that in love, as in other matters, the young are just beginners, and that the art of love matures with age and experience.'[1]

It may seem that everybody knows what love is, but if we ask people what they mean by the term, a wide variety of answers will be given. People form their concepts of the nature of love according to their own experience and that of their friends and acquaintances. They are also influenced by the way love is commonly presented by the media and how literature and art has represented love throughout the ages. People's knowledge of books may not be at first hand. Thus someone may never have read Shakespeare or seen his plays performed, but as the views of so important an author have influenced subsequent writers, playwrights, poets, novelists and broadcasters, so the outlook of us all owes something to his work.

If we consult the works of influential writers it is evident that there is very little consensus. Is love always associated with jealousy? Is genuine love of a very enduring nature? Is it a matter of almost instant attraction, as evident in *Romeo and Juliet*, or does true love develop slowly out of friendship? Do both sexes love in much the same way or is love a very different phenomenon for men and for women? Is love in later life much the same as love in our youth? A host of such questions arise when we turn to literature.

From ancient times many writers have held that extreme jealousy is a necessary characteristic of love, but Margaret Mead, writing in modern times, wrote, 'Jealousy is not a barometer by which depth of love can be read; it merely records the degree of the lover's insecurity.'[2] In one of Shakespeare's well-known sonnets the enduring nature of love is stressed:

> Love is not love
> Which alters when it alteration finds,
> Or bends with the remover to remove:
> O, no! It is an ever-fixed mark,
> That looks on tempests and is never shaken;
> It is a star to every wandering bark,
> Whose worth's unknown, although his height be taken.
> Love's not Time's fool, though rosy lips and cheeks
> Within his bending sickle's compass come . . .[3]

By contrast, the poems of Swinburne generally stress the impermanent quality of love: 'Laurel is green for a season, and love is sweet for a day . . .'[4]

Bizet's opera *Carmen* concerns the passionate love of a gypsy girl who loves suddenly and intensely but who soon changes her affections, claiming that:

> Love is like any wood-bird wild
> That one can never hope to tame.[5]

We may wonder how many women have tried to model their style of loving after the example of Carmen and felt that this was really how love should be. In Verdi's opera *Rigoletto* the Duke sings of the essential inconstancy of women's love, and Byron claims that loving is essentially different for the two sexes:

> Man's love is of man's life a thing apart,
> 'Tis woman's whole existence.[6]

One could quote many contradictory statements that have been made about love. William Blake's poem 'The Clod and the Pebble' presents two fundamentally different concepts of love:

> Love seeketh not itself to please,
> Nor for itself hath any care,
> But for another gives its ease
> And builds a Heaven in Hell's despair . . .

> Love seeketh only Self to please
> To bind another to its delight,
> Joys in another's loss of ease
> And builds a Hell in Heaven's despite.[7]

It is apparent that there are several different types of love, and people are referring to disparate things but alluding to them all as 'love'. It is possible that when we are old we may love in one way rather than another, and the incredulity with which younger people sometimes regard the love of elderly people may be due to a confusion over terms. Let us take a look at the ideas people have had about love throughout the ages.

Types of love

At the level of common sense most people would agree that there are two types of love: that which includes an erotic component, as between lovers and husbands and wives, and that which does not, as between parents and children, family members and very dear friends. The term 'erotic' derives from the Greek god Eros and implies sexual passion and physical contact and caressing, yet here we encounter an anomaly. Some non-sexual love is also expressed in physical touching and caressing, as when a father gives his infant son a kiss and a cuddle. It is perfectly rational and desirable for parents to express their love of young children by physical caresses, but there is no sexual arousal involved where normal people are concerned. Yet it is of interest to consider how convention determines that such physical contact shall be phased out as the child grows older. In Anglo-American culture a father will love his adolescent son as much as he did when the boy was a toddler yet generally he will no longer cuddle and kiss him. It is rather different for the mother; she will usually retain a greater degree of physical expression of affection for her son when he grows older.

The kiss is the last vestige of non-sexual physical contact between those who love or who have affection (which is what we call a minor degree of love) for one another. But it is nevertheless sexually determined: I may kiss the wife of an old friend as a greeting but I do not kiss him, I shake his hand. This is the limit of our physical contact, as we are heterosexual. Some women friends will greet me with a kiss on the cheek and others with a kiss on the lips, surely a more erotic greeting. Perhaps they do this because I am an old man and hence less likely to make a sexual pass at them; they would be less likely to do it to a young man. There are many variants on such customs in other countries and, indeed, in our own history there have been times when male friends would kiss one another, as some female friends do today, and it was not thought at all odd among heterosexuals.

A common distinction between the two main types of love is the 'erotic' and the 'platonic', the latter term deriving from the philosophical writings of Plato. Here a huge misunderstanding is involved, because the ideas of Plato about sex, eroticism and love are so far removed from those of our Western Christian heritage that it is very difficult for us to comprehend them. His ideas were formed in a society where women were of little account and mature men were commonly involved in some degree of pederastic love with adolescent boys. Plato equated 'the Good' with 'the Beautiful' and held that 'Eros is the reaching out of the soul for a hoped for good'.[8] He was concerned that men should put spiritual and intellectual preoccupations above their sheer bodily indulgence but showed a surprising tolerance for pederastic love. I think that it is best that we should avoid the confusions engendered by the term 'platonic love'.

A number of writers have considered how many types of love there are and proposed their own schemes.

The theme of love enters into many of Chaucer's works and he embraces it in all its manifestations, contrasting the ideal of courtly love with that of earthy eroticism so well expounded by the Wife of Bath. He identifies three types: courtly love which is essentially romantic; natural love, which leads to and persists in marriage; and sheer erotic indulgence. These three kinds of love are exemplified in many of his poems and tales. Chaucer's popularity both in his own time and ever since is largely due to the fact that his writings appeal to all kinds of readers: those of refined literary tastes and those who want a good, rumbustious and often bawdy tale. We shall return to Chaucer when we consider the theme of old love in literature.

C. S. Lewis's book *The Four Loves* is probably little known today because his type of male-dominated, pipe-smoking, beer-swilling Christianity is very much out of favour.[9] He named his four types Affection, Friendship, Eros and Charity and grouped together the first three as 'natural loves'. The fourth, Charity, he referred to in terms of his concept of the loving relationship which he thought should obtain between God and Man.

Lewis's concept of Affection is very simple and is that which is generally held. Many writers have referred to it by the Greek word storge and most dictionaries refer to storgic love as that which parents naturally feel for their children. He makes the point that this type of love is sometimes fulfilled by an affectionate relationship with a domestic pet. This observation should not be neglected in relation to many older people in the modern world, where the break-up of the family has resulted in men and women who have outlived most of their family and friends being dependent on a relationship with a dog or cat.

It is when Lewis comes to discuss Friendship that his book may strike the modern reader as strange and we become conscious of the extent to which his own very unusual love life has influenced his thinking. He writes entirely from the standpoint of a man and even doubts whether friendship can exist between men and women. He writes, 'From what has been said it will be clear that in most societies at most periods Friendships will be between men and men or between women and women. The sexes will have met one another in Affection and in Eros but not in this love. For they will seldom have had with each other the companionship in common activities which is the matrix of Friendship.'

As is well known, Lewis tended to get together with an all-male clique known as the 'Inklings' and women were normally excluded from their social gatherings. The chapter on Friendship contains a lengthy repudiation of the suggestion that love between men may imply homosexuality, and some may think that indeed he protests too much and was merely resisting admitting that there was a strongly homosexual element in the association between him and his friends, a suggestion that was quite taboo at the time.

These days, when men and women have become less sensitive about homosexuality, people are relatively unconcerned as to whether their friendships contain a degree of erotic attraction and less prone to separate a 'man's world' from a 'woman's world' so categorically. This may not be so true of the older generations who are now entering the Third Age, and they may have more diffi-culty in later life. In this connection the autobiographical accounts of the late loves of Harriet and Charlie given in Part 2 are particularly apposite.

By Eros, Lewis means what is generally known as falling in love. He fully admits the component of sexuality in this phenomenon but points out that there can be sexual desire without this falling in love, a fact that is generally acknowledged. However, Lewis goes further and says that in Eros the sexual component may not be recognized or important.

If this were true and the desire involved in falling in love is not necessarily sexually toned, then a man may equally fall in love with another man yet not be homosexual, thus Lewis's distinction between Friendship and Eros breaks down. He seems unaware of this point.

One of the main problems about Lewis's advice concerning love that he offers so confidently to other people is that he had so peculiar a love life himself. Most of his ideas come from reading and not from actual personal experience. He spent almost the whole of his adult life living with a woman who was twenty-five years his senior and he would never clarify whether or not she was his mistress. In writing of Lewis, John Carey refers to the fact that 'for most of his adult life he worked as unpaid housemaid and errand boy for a tyrannical lady'[10] and this perhaps explains his great interest in the medieval knights who served their ladies for so long and so abjectly. Late in his fifties he married Joy Davidman and enjoyed a brief life with her before she died, but there are some who question whether this marriage was ever consummated.

Some of Lewis's attitudes towards sex will not commend themselves to many modern readers. He was strongly in favour of bawdry and used to encourage his male English students to attend parties where they were expected to get drunk and sing bawdy songs. Lewis believed that sex was a joke that the Almighty had seen fit to visit on man. Carnal things, Lewis believed, were best regarded in the light of St Francis's statement that the body was 'Brother Ass'.

Lewis's fourth definition of love, which he called Charity, may dismay many Christians. Theologians have maintained that he was simply confused when he tried to write about theology. What he means by Charity is what others call by the Greek word *agape*. By Charity we generally mean what is defined in the dictionary as 'Christian love; especially the Christian love of our fellow men',[11] but this is precisely what Lewis does not mean. He argued that the three natural loves are in competition with the love that Man should feel for God. He therefore believed that the three natural loves should be if not actually suppressed at least 'transformed' in the service of the greater love for God. In this sense we should restrict the love that we normally feel for those closest to us in order to love God more perfectly.

It may seem strange to pay so much attention here to a writer who is so much out of tune with modern views about love and sex today, but his views were influential in the 1960s and he was a popular broadcaster. People who are now in the Third Age may have had their views about love affected by him in the past and he certainly influenced some later writers such as Rollo May, an American existentialist psychiatrist who also put forward his own scheme of Four Loves a decade later in his book *Love and Will*.[12] May's definitions are not sufficiently distinctive to warrant discussion in detail. He differed from Lewis in that he did not impose on them an eccentric theological view but, reacting against what he regarded as the extreme permissiveness of the 1960s, tended to uphold a rather stern moralistic attitude.

The approach of John Lee may commend itself to older people who are facing problems in coming to terms with the modern world and who are having to reassess some beliefs and attitudes that they adopted in their formative years.[13] In the autobiographical account given in Part 2 by Cecily, she tells how, when she left her husband as she was approaching the age of sixty and settled in a new town, she was surprised by the new doctor she consulted on a health problem. This doctor, a woman not much different from her in age, inquired about matters related to her future sex life. Cecily found it 'bizarre' that anyone should ask about this aspect of life at her 'advanced' age, having taken it for granted that now she had left her husband she could never expect to have an erotic relationship again. In fact, after a few years she fell in love and formed a very satisfactory sexual partnership. She had been perfectly prepared to form new friendships and affections, but she did not understand the nature of love in its various manifestations.

Harriet, previously a wife and mother and quite prepared to settle in a quiet retired life, having drifted away from her husband, found herself falling most erotically in love with another woman and settling into a very successful lesbian partnership. Tina, having formed a stable relationship with an elderly man and expecting this relationship to turn into marriage, found after a lapse of a few years that age does not, as is conventionally believed, quell the roving sexual habits of some men. Gertrude's husband, bereaved in his sixties, took the sensible step of remarrying, only to find that his children became implacably hostile and disowned him. Monica, meanwhile, examined her new relationship with a man and asked, 'Is this love?' The world is changing and it seems that we have to take a new look at love.

John Lee has an unusual approach to dealing with the problem of trying to understand and delineate the nature of love. He points out that the ancient Greeks and Romans used different words for various types of love but did not insist that one type was superior to another, just as they set up altars to different gods but each was accorded equal respect. This approach, he contends, was destroyed by Christianity, which insisted that there was only one true God and one true and superior form of love. This tendency is exemplified at its extreme by C. S. Lewis. Lee points out that in modern times we are beginning to go back to the tolerance and pluralism of the classical age and we are coming to accept the equal validity of what he refers to as different 'lovestyles'.

Lee points out that authors who write about love have generally gathered their ideas from previous authors and combined them with insights gained from their own personal experience. Such an approach has been useful, and contemporary beliefs about love have been influenced by such authors as Somerset Maugham and D. H. Lawrence. People who read their books relate the authors' ideas to their own lives and form opinions about the essential nature of love but sometimes come to entirely different conclusions.

Rollo May and other therapists have based their ideas on long experience with people who have come to them with their troubles. Although psychiatrists may arrive at many important insights about loving, we may ask how valid such accounts are compared to what Lee calls the 'many happy, lazy or pedestrian affairs' that never come to the attention of the therapist. Apart from psychiatrists, psychologists and marriage counsellors, sociologists have sometimes approached the problem of love, but they generally begin by picking on one definition of love and thus exclude large areas of human experience from their attempts to explain the role of love in society. Others choose to define two types of love, romantic and realistic, and then leave us in little doubt as to what they consider to be real love.

Lee's approach is that of a scientist; that is, first collecting a huge number of observations and then developing a theory on the basis of the accumulating evidence and testing that theory. He describes his initial procedure:

> I began sorting out ideas about love into types by collecting over 4000 statements from the fictional and non-fictional literature of love, including Plato and the Bible, Doris Lessing and D. H. Lawrence, romantic Lord Byron and cynical La Rochefoucauld. All the statements were then cross-classified according to such topics as jealousy, altruism and physical beauty. [14]

He found that some common themes began to emerge. Whereas some writers such as St Paul and Erich Fromm considered love to be a universal quality, others maintained that love was jealous, possessive and essentially concerned with one beloved person. He called to his assistance people in the fields of literature, psychology and philosophy and by their efforts they reduced his list of thousands of statements to just thirty, which dealt with six basic themes. From this list he devised a questionnaire to see what kinds of love were most commonly agreed on.

Not everyone will agree with this method of working, for questionnaires may lead to all sorts of false conclusions in research, but at least it formed a basis on which to proceed. In fact his initial research led to many difficulties, for the same person might agree with some quite contrary statements about love. For example, someone might maintain that the love in a 'shipboard romance' (where two people love one another for a few days and then part for good) was genuine love but also agree with the statement that the only way to know whether love is genuine is to test it over a long period of time. In following up these questionnaires by interviews, he found that people were able to explain such obvious contradictions, generally saying something like

'It depends on what kind of love you mean.' People seemed to know instinctively that they recognized quite different forms of love as being genuine but were at a loss to put names to these different types.

It is to Lee's credit that he avoided using the most usual categories of people who feature so widely in published research studies – the university student and the therapist's client – and approached the ordinary man and woman in the street. He constructed an interview method in which a complete stranger could explain in an organized way what happened when he or she was in a relationship defined as love. He covered quite a wide range of events in the interviewee's life: recollections of childhood, feelings about work, close friends, self-esteem and life in general at the start of a love affair. He asked about people's expectations of love, their ideals and how they met their loved ones. He was, of course, dependent on the truthfulness and frankness of those he interviewed, but there is a good deal of evidence obtained from wide areas of research that people are generally prepared to be remarkably frank with a stranger, provided that he or she is perceived as being trustworthy and unlikely to make improper use of confidences. In these interviews people reported on their thoughts and behaviour while away from the loved one, the nature and timing of their sexual intimacy if any, experiences of jealousy and the frequency and nature of rows if any. They discussed break-ups and reunions, love triangles, homosexual relationships, serial love affairs, simultaneous involvements and many other aspects of loving.

From this research three basic kinds of love emerged and all other types of love seemed to be variations on these. Lee considers that each love relationship can be described in terms of a 'lovestyle' and the following quotation gives his description of the three primary varieties.

Eros
This is the ancient Greek term for love fascinated by ideal images of beauty. This lovestyle is the search for the one perfect beloved.

Ludus
This is the Latin word for play or game. It was first used by the
Roman poet Ovid in the year AD1 to describe a love that would
rather be playful than serious. Any number can play.

Storge
The ancient Greeks used this word for the natural affection that
develops between close brothers and sisters or childhood friends.
This is an affectionate, companionate style of loving.

One may criticize Lee's definition of Eros, for in the history of
ancient Greece the concept of Eros changed. Originally Eros was
the god of passion and fertility, but in the Platonic Dialogues Eros
is no longer considered as a god but as a creative force. Certainly
in our language the term erotic is more strongly linked with sexual
passion than with any ideal of beauty. The beloved who is loved
erotically may not be perceived as specially beautiful, although he
or she may have qualities that transcend mere physical beauty. Lee
states that 'An immediate, powerful attraction to the physical
appearance of the beloved is the typical symptom of Eros', and it
may be noted that he refers to 'attraction' rather than stressing
physical beauty. This is important to appreciate when considering
people who fall in love in later life. The attractive person may be
grey and wrinkled and not at all conforming to the usual standards
of beauty.

The method of procedure in Lee's research seems justified by
the fact that he did not stick to his original assumptions but mod-
ified his views as the result of the many interviews he conducted.
He writes:

I began with the suspicion that Eros was little more than a
projection of the lover's imagination on to a suitable object: 'There
is a period of thrill, anticipation, and tension, then a period of

acquaintance, enjoyment and ecstasy, then a decline into disenchantment,' I noted at the time. I expected Eros to be superficial,
motivated mainly by the sexual drive, and quickly exhausted . . .
Interviews with actual lovers changed my mind. I uncovered stories of 'love at first sight' whose initial rapture survived years of life
together.[15]

He goes on to note that in successful and enduring erotic
relationships the first excitement of attraction was followed by
more profound physical rapport, the lovers speaking of delight in
the smell, skin surface, hair texture, bodily proportions and
other physical features. We shall see later in the present book
that some people in later life – in their sixties and seventies –
report this feature of physical delight in their lovers' time-worn
bodies. In Lee's experience, physical attraction serves as the driving power toward psychological rapport in love relationships
that are truly erotic. We may be reminded here of Donne's poem
The Ecstasie:

> So must pure lovers' souls descend
> T'affections and to faculties,
> Which sense may reach and apprehend,
> Else a great prince in prison lies.
>
> To our bodies turn we then, that so
> Weak men on love revealed may look;
> Love's mysteries in souls do grow,
> But yet the body is his book.[16]

In making a good deal of Ovid's Ludus, Lee reflects a trend that
has been growing in the post-war 'permissive society'. Ovid's
works were generally honoured in medieval and Renaissance
times, but his amoral attitude to sexual love brought about a reac-

tion early in the nineteenth century. In 1805 the critic William Preston complained that Ovid was one of the first to spoil:

the pure taste of the Romans. He is lavish in flowers and ornaments, in sallies of imagination, in conceits and points of wit; in his morality he is most relaxed and vicious . . . Many of his subjects are licentious, many immoral, in the highest degree, and not only in scattered passages, but entire compositions are such, as are highly offensive to decency and must shock the modest reader.[17]

The general prudery of the nineteenth century outlawed Ovid's ludic attitude to amatory behaviour, at least in public profession. There are certainly many people today who would say 'But that behaviour is not love', thus claiming that their own definition of love is exclusive and is the only proper one. However, throughout most of European history ludic amatory behaviour has definitely been regarded as one form of love and it seems perverse to deny it. The general objection to ludic love is that people do not always confine their love games to partners who are similarly inclined. If a partner in an affair or a long-term relationship is looking for committed erotic love or settled storgic love, he or she may get badly hurt emotionally. Ovid's advice in the *Ars Amatoria* was frankly cynical: we should play an elaborate part like an actor in order to achieve our ends. This may lead to outright deception in some cases where the partner is naive or wilfully blind to the real nature of their lover's approach. The unwilling partner may use every tactic that he or she can employ to change the behaviour and outlook of the ludic lover to a lovestyle that is more acceptable. The ludic lovers, for their part, may feel that they must take good care not to get trapped into a permanent relationship where their freedom is sacrificed.

Lee uses the Greek word *storge* to describe an 'affectionate, companionate style of loving'. There is very little difference between the various theorists about this type of love. Although an element of *storge* is typical of most lovers, in the sexual sense, it also typifies many loving relationships in which there is little or no element of sexuality. C. S. Lewis refers to the fact that, in general, we love people because of their positive attributes, but here is a form of affection that often exists in spite of, rather than because of, many of the less desirable personal characteristics of the loved one. A striking example of this is given by Monica in Part 2 in her account of her relationship with Peter, whom she describes as perfectly 'awful' and utterly different from herself: 'Wendy Cope said that there are so many kinds of awful men, and he certainly has one kind of awfulness I never encountered before.'

Storge tends to grow with time and to be associated with everyday, comfortable familiarity. Lee refers to the fact that some marriages are essentially storgic and says, 'One playful affair in which you wandered from the straight and narrow of a storgic marriage does not make you henceforth a ludic lover.' He refers to the fact that parents' love for their children is normally storgic and questions the validity of jealousy and cheating when someone loves simultaneously two (or more) people with a different lovestyle. Thus if someone loves his wife erotically, it would be odd to suggest that he is cheating on her because he loves his children storgically. Jealousy may arise when an attachment occurs outside the family, because most people have only one concept of love and imagine that there is a finite quantity of it available which cannot be divided legitimately. Hence the term cheating is used. It is possible that a husband or wife who is frustrated erotically might actually feel jealous of the storgic love that is given to the family cat, but most people would regard this as highly abnormal.

We will discuss later the general and traditional assumption that the love between people in later life must be entirely storgic; hence such poems as 'John Anderson My Jo'[18] and the ideal of Darby and Joan. Lee's position is that, with certain modifications, a loving relationship can be classed as one lovestyle or another. This assumption is questionable, particularly as concerns storgic love, for it is hardly possible to conceive of any relationship other than a one-night stand that does not contain some element of *storge*.

Lee uses the analogy of colour to explain his three-part division of lovestyles and the first edition of his book had the title *Colours of Love: An Exploration of the Ways of Loving.*[19] He points out that there are only three basic hues: red, yellow and blue. All others are produced by varying combinations of the three primary colours. He then goes on to make the case that there are secondary types of lovestyles, such as 'ludic eros', 'storgic eros' and 'storgic ludus'.

The analogy of the different colours is not wholly satisfactory. For instance, Lee admits that there is a form of love known as *agape* and refers to St Paul's letter to the Corinthians. Above I have quoted from William Blake and the first verse of his poem might well be a description of true *agape*: 'Love seeketh not itself to please'. The interviews that Lee conducted did not reveal a single case of pure agapic love and he admits that it is difficult to see how *agape* can be a secondary form of love derived from two of the primary lovestyles. At best, it may be suggested that *agape* is a combination of Eros and *storge*. It may draw its intensity and power from Eros but, as in *storge*, overlooks the many faults and imperfections of the loved one with patience and self-restraint. As complete *agape* may be impossible for any human being it may be regarded simply as an ideal. Although none of the interviews revealed a form of love that was simply *agape*, some loves might be characterized as 'near-*agape*'.

An interesting interview is mentioned which concerned a man who, out of unselfish and self-sacrificing concern for his beloved, disappeared out of her life for several months because she was emotionally torn between her love for him and for another man who might have brought her more happiness. One of the men had to be hurt and he elected to take the hurt upon himself. However, this man's action fell short of pure *agape* because he was interested in how his beloved was getting on with her new partner and could not help being rather pleased when he heard that they were quarrelling. Eventually, to his joy, this association broke up and the woman, realizing that his action had been motivated by real concern for her, chose him as the better partner.

The discussion of separate and combined lovestyles which Lee presents is highly complex and even involves tertiary lovestyles as well as secondary. We need not discuss his theories any further here but simply accepting the proposal that there are three separate lovestyles gives us a working basis on which to consider love in later life.

Lovestyles in later life

We may now consider how people will change in later life as to their manner of loving. Will they love as they always have or will ageing bring about fundamental changes in their lovestyle? It is traditionally assumed that in later life the only form of love that is manifest is storgic, however the individual may have loved in the younger years. In Yeats's poem 'When You Are Old' he writes of the ageing woman:

> And bending down beside the glowing bars,
> Murmur, a little sadly, how love fled
> And paced upon the mountains overhead,
> And hid his face amid a cloud of stars.

Does love inevitably have to fly away in this manner simply because we are old?

The idea that ludic love is most inappropriate in our later years is very widely accepted. In Shakespeare's *Merry Wives of Windsor* Falstaff is mocked and eventually humiliated because he attempts to love erotically in a ludic manner. Older men who show an interest in erotic love are sometimes called 'dirty old men'. But traditional assumptions are sometimes wrong, particularly when society has changed as radically as it has in the twentieth century.

Love in youth and old age

The various kinds of love that are expressed throughout adult life have been described, but there is a further division that should be considered: the significance of loving in the younger and older years of our lives. In our younger years although we do not make love sexually purely for the purpose of procreation, in its broadest sense it may be considered 'generative love': a love of our partner, family, home and hearth, a love of children, a love that is important for the future of society. This generative love is manifest in all animal species. They do not know the meaning of mating behaviour which may in its early stages be purely ludic, but it leads on to the eroticism of their couplings and the storgic love manifest in the rearing of their offspring.

In later life, when we are no longer concerned with procreation, our love may be called 'existential love' and it is an essentially human attribute. It reflects the poignant awareness that our existence is transient, that we are aware in our Third Age of what is expressed in the *Rubáiyát of Omar Khayyám*:

> The bird of Time but has a little way
> To fly, and Lo! – the bird is on the wing.

This distinction between generative and existential love has been pointed out in the work of two Swedish authors, Nancy Datan and Dean Rodeheaver, who write:

We believe that existential love, the capacity to cherish the present moment, is one of the greatest gifts of maturity. Perhaps we first learn this love when we first confront the certainty of our own personal death, most often in middle adulthood. Generative love is characteristic of parenthood, a time during which sacrifices are gladly made for the sake of children. However, it is existential love, we feel, that creates the unique patience and tenderness so often seen in grandparents, who know how brief the period of childhood is, since they have seen their own children leave childhood behind them.[20]

Present-day society is only just beginning to awaken to the potential for existential love between older men and women and only recently have we acknowledged the pleasures of sexuality as belonging to the whole natural life-span, particularly in the later years.

It has long been accepted in the romantic tradition that young people are ready to 'die for love' as it can be very important in their youthful lives, and a great deal of literature has been written on this theme. Consider, however, the following sort of tragedy: in an old people's home a man and a woman fell in love, a passion that no one took very seriously. The old man's children thought that this late-life flowering of passion was 'cute', but the woman's children thought it was disgraceful and, despite her protests, they removed her from the home. A month later, although apparently healthy, she registered her final protest: she died. Such a case is by no means unique and it is significant that love leading to death has been the subject of much great tragic literature but only when the protagonists are young. It might be said that if Romeo had lost his Juliet he could easily have found another girl and become equally impassioned with her, but an old lady in an old people's home or living with her disapproving family would have practically no chance of ever finding another lover. Is not the latter case the greater tragedy?

In the younger years of life people have many forms of satisfaction: their work, their sports, their rich social lives, their innumerable opportunities for active pursuits. It is in the later years that existential love begins to take on a special importance and, as observed by Monica, one of the contributors to this book,'My conclusion on love in later life is that we cannot afford to deny it, whatever its imperfections. It may be of a kind we should have never considered in earlier more idealistic days, but now we must enjoy what we may while we may.'

CHAPTER 2

Late love in literature

Although some people may not have read much literature, we have all been influenced by what has been written throughout the ages. The curious fact about the theme of love and eroticism in later life is that it hardly exists. Although people have been falling in love, making love and enjoying and suffering all that goes with it in the later years of life for millennia, this has been hardly noticed and little commented on, at least in Western Christendom.

One reason for this obvious neglect is that in the past there were relatively few old people in society and that those still alive were often in poor health. It is only in the last half of the twentieth century that we have seen the emergence of a significant number of elderly people who are still relatively healthy and active. Another reason for this neglect in literature is that part of the *Zeitgeist* of Christian civilization has been to deny to older people much of a significant role to play in society.

The Bible
The Bible is one of the best-known and most influential literary works. One must draw a distinction between the Old Testament and the New. In the former it was not at all strange for older people to be sexually active. Many of the prophets went on cohabiting with their wives and concubines in old age, even begetting children. Solomon, when old and sick, had a young woman brought to his bed to bring back his strength, and the eroticism of

naughty old men was depicted in the story of Susannah and the Elders. I know of no instances of the eroticism of older women being recognized in the Old Testament, but then the Jewish tradition was extremely male oriented.

The New Testament was not primarily Jewish in inspiration and it arose in a reaction to the libertine pagan culture of the Graeco-Roman world. It is full of such injunctions as 'That the aged men be sober, grave, temperate, sound in faith, in charity, in patience. The aged women likewise, that they be in behaviour as becometh holiness.' The general idea was that the elderly should spend whatever time was left to them in self-abasement and preparation for death. Shakespeare ends his play *The Tempest* with the elderly Prospero saying, with all Christian humility, 'And thence retire me to my Milan, where every third thought shall be my grave.' We would consider this to be a rather morbid preoccupation for an elderly person today.

The Graeco-Roman world

The fact that older people have erotic needs, fall in love and form new relationships has been almost wholly ignored in literature throughout the Christian era, but this was not so among the ancient Greeks. In Aristophanes's play *Ecclesiazusae* there is an honest recognition of the fact that many women have a need for erotic love when they are old, just as they have when they are young.[1] This play is a brutal satire but nevertheless recognizes the realities of life. The theme is that the women of Athens have taken over the government and, recognizing the need of elderly women for a sex life, they introduce a law decreeing that no young man can have his girlfriend without first giving sexual service to any elderly woman who is attracted to him. Three women, identified as 'hags', lust after the same young man and prevent him from getting together with his girlfriend. Despite its coarse theme it shows that in ancient Greece they acknowledged a fact that is only beginning to be acknowledged today: that age makes very little difference to a woman's erotic inclinations.

A more humane view in classical literature is taken by such writers as the Greek lyric poet Philodemus. He celebrates the erotic capacity of older women:

> Charito is more than sixty
> Yet her hair is still a dense forest
> No brassière holds up the marble cones
> Of her high-pointed breasts.
> Her unwrinkled flesh exhales ambrosia
> And myriads of teasing charms.
> Lovers, if you do not run from hot desire,
> Enjoy Charito
> And forget her many decades.[2]

Here the poet Philodemus displays a macho male's attitude to female sexuality, in that he praises Charito simply because she resembles a younger woman; he misses the point about what constitutes attractiveness in older women. An older woman can still be attractive when she no longer has high-pointed breasts and an unwrinkled skin. The attractiveness of an older person lies in the character of the face, which can still be striking and charming despite the many wrinkles, and an attractive personality is conveyed by the whole body. As the sixteenthpoet John Donne put it:

> No spring, nor summer beauty hath such grace,
> As I have seen in one autumnal face.[3]

There was certainly an ambiguity in the attitudes to sexuality in later life in the ancient classical world and the idea that it should be a time of renunciation of erotic love finds some expression among the philosophers. In Plato's *The Republic* we read:

> I was once present when someone was asking the poet Sophocles about sex, and whether he was still able to make love to a woman; to which he replied, 'Don't talk about that; I have left it behind me and escaped from the madness and slavery of passion.' A good reply I thought then, and still do. For in old age you become quite free of passions of this sort and they leave you in peace.[4]

But as both Sophocles and Plato were reputed to have adolescent boys as their loves in their peaceful old age, their retirement from heterosexual hurly-burly may not mean quite what many people think of as platonic love.

The medieval Church

In the Middle Ages the Church exerted a strong influence on what it was permissible to write. According to St Augustine, the dominant thinker in the Western Christian Church of the fifth century, the ideal was celibacy, and within marriage sexual activity was moral only if it were for the purpose of procreation. After the age of child-bearing, therefore, it was most improper for women to have sex. The general attitude was that for older men to show erotic interest was to invite ridicule but for women it was positively evil.

Despite Church teaching there were periods during the Middle Ages in which there were outbreaks of sexual libertinism, and in the fifteenth century there was a major effort by the ecclesiastical authorities to repress both heresy and witchcraft. *The Malleus Maleficarum* (the Hammer of Witches) was published in 1486 and, according to this treatise, sexual acts were indicative of witchcraft, as all witchcraft was due to carnal lusts. It was held that witches were characterized by an insatiable sexual appetite and set out to tempt and ruin men. Historians tell us, however, that during the Middle Ages there were in fact enormous contradictions between what was preached and prevailing sexual practices.

Geoffrey Chaucer

Much of our literature in Britain has been strongly influenced by Chaucer, the most prolific writer of the fourteenth century. He in turn looked to the writers of Renaissance Italy such as Boccaccio, who generally adhered to the convention of condemning erotic love in later life, and when the theme occurs it is generally the subject of farce.

In Chaucer's *Merchant's Tale* the 'old' knight January (who was sixty years old) marries a young woman May and is cuckolded by her and made a fool of in a grotesquely comic way. By studying this tale we may get a good picture of the medieval attitudes towards sex. The theme of rich old men making use of their wealth to marry younger women occurs throughout Chaucer's works. The character states his preference for younger women thus:

> Flesh should be young though fish should be mature;
> A pike, not pickerel, makes the tastier meal
> Old beef is not so good as tender veal.
> I'll have no woman thirty years of age –
> That's only fodder, bean-straw for a cage.[5]

It should be noted that January is depicted as wanting sex rather than love in his ageing life but desires it in a manner that was respectable according to Church teaching:

> And blessed be the yoke that we are in
> For nothing that we can do will count as sin.
> A man is not a sinner with his wife,
> He cannot hurt himself with his own knife.

January is warned by his friends that he may be cuckolded if he takes a young wife but, nothing daunted despite his white hair, he boasts of his own prowess:

> I may seem hoary, but I am like a tree
> That blossoms white before the fruit can be;
> Blossoming trees are neither dry nor dead
> And I am only hoary on my head.
> My heart and all my members are as green
> As laurel is; all the year round I mean.

However, his young wife May falls in love with his young servant Damian and after January goes blind they plan to have a secret love affair. Their first coupling takes place in a pear tree in January's garden with him dozing beneath, but this monstrous affront to male dignity urges Pluto, the king of the fairies, to take a hand and he restores January's sight so that he can see what the lovers are doing above him. When he accuses May of this gross betrayal she succeeds in convincing him that in recovering his sight he can only see partially and in a distorted manner to begin with, so that what he thinks he saw was not really true. Thus the tale not only bears the message that 'old' men should not seek carnal solace with young wives but that females are so cunning that they can bamboozle their husbands in the most brazen manner.

Nevertheless, Chaucer's attitude to love in later life was equivocal and challenged the official teaching of the Church on the subject. In the 'Prologue to the Wife of Bath's Tale' he speaks up for the rights of women in a most surprising way. This formidable old lady has outlived five husbands yet, despite the loss of her youthful beauty, she still boldly declares that she will welcome a husband and challenges the official doctrine on sex:

Virginity is great perfection,
And continence also with devotion,
But Christ, that of perfection is a well,
Bade not every man that he should sell
All that he had, and give it to the poor
And in suchwise follow through his door.
He spoke to those who would live perfectly;
And lordlings, by your leave, that I'm not.
I will bestow the flower of all my life
In the acts and fruits of a wife . . .

Let them be bread of pure white seed,
And let us wives known as barley-bread;
And yet with barley bread Mark can tell
Our Lord Jesus refreshed men as well
In such estate as God has called us
I'll stay as I'm not precious.
In wifehood will I use my instrument
As freely as my Maker has it sent.
If I be grudging, God give me sorrow!
My husband shall it have both eve and morrow
When he wants to come and pay his debt . . .

Alas, alas that ever love was sin!
I followed aye my inclination
By virtue of my constellation
That made me; I could not withdraw
My chamber of Venus from a good fellow.[6]

Such frank admission of a sexual appetite in an older woman does not appear to awaken disapproval in the group of other pilgrims, which included some churchmen and nuns who appear to accept her for what she is.

Shakespeare and later writers

Shakespeare has a generally negative attitude towards older people showing erotic interest and, like Chaucer, mocks older men who want sex. In *The Merry Wives of Windsor* Falstaff is led on by the two sprightly wives simply for the purpose of humiliating him. The message is that old men should not aspire to the prerogatives of youth and, if they fall prey to the pranks of younger women, it serves them right. Elsewhere Shakespeare writes, 'Age I do abhor thee, youth I do adore thee'.[7] We hear of our present age being referred to as being 'youth oriented', but it seems that this is nothing new. It is in the famous bedchamber scene in *Hamlet* that Shakespeare makes his hero condemn most bitterly his mother going to bed to make love with her second husband Claudius, his uncle, and he states that he thinks that a woman of her age should be finished with such things.

In later literature sexism is often combined with ageism and it is women who are specially condemned if they show erotic interest in later life. This theme arises in Restoration comedy, as in Congreve's *Way of the World*, where the ageing Lady Wishfort (note the name!) is ridiculed because she falls in love with Mirabell.

In the novels of Charles Dickens there are several examples of older women being cruelly mocked. We can sympathize with poor Madelene Bray in *Nicholas Nickleby*, whose selfish father wishes to marry her to the horrible old Arthur Gride. This 'selling off' of young women to elderly bachelors was probably a not uncommon practice in Victorian England. But when Dickens introduces the case of an older woman contemplating a love affair he becomes positively vitriolic. It is said that he was representing his own mother as Mrs Nickleby and presents a cruel picture of her believing that the man next door has fallen in love with her, while it is evident that the poor man is hopelessly insane and the methods of his wooing are utterly grotesque. Whether Mrs Dickens ever did have such a passion in later life is unknown, but Charles Dickens uses the theme for a general satire on older women. Madam La Crevy and Flora Finching are mocked because despite their age they are attracted to a man.

If we consider twentieth-century writers, such as Colette, Thomas Hardy, Henrik Ibsen, Henry James, D. H. Lawrence, Somerset Maugham, Marcel Proust and George Bernard Shaw, who have written a good deal about the theme of love and sex, they largely ignore the fact that people can fall in love in later life and that such love can be as meaningful as love in youth and middle age. This is curious, as in their own lives many of them encountered examples of newly formed love relationships among people of quite advanced age. It is true that Ibsen used the theme of an old man falling in love with a young woman in his play *The Master Builder* and this was partly autobiographical and related to his own attachment to Emilie Bardach, a young Viennese woman whom he described as his 'May sun in a September life'. It will be remembered that the Master Builder fell to his death whilst trying to show off to his youthful love, but Ibsen avoided any such fate by breaking off relations with Emilie in his old age.

An American writer, Professor Don Charles, has conducted a painstaking review of literature from the Old Testament onwards to discover how frequently old people are mentioned. He found that their presence was very infrequent and, where they did occur, they were in somewhat unimportant roles. He notes that in literature after the seventeenth century the single old character who has 'any apparent sex drive' was Old Tom, or Grampa, in John Steinbeck's *Grapes of Wrath*, an old man who is 'lean, ragged, mischievous and lecherous'. Professor Charles went on to search what he describes as 'other fiction': light novels of the past century written for a wide readership, including romances, westerns and magazine fiction. In them there are many that include old people as protagonists or major characters. He writes, 'These old people tend to be treated sympathetically and sentimentally; they are oppressed, neglected, tragic, occasionally strong and succorant. However, they are rarely powerful, achieving figures and are never "tainted" by sex![8]

Modern literature

In modern literature there are signs that this neglect of older people and their loves is changing. Several writers have discussed the extent to which older characters are given prominence in modern fiction and where the validity of erotic interest and need in such people can be admitted and, indeed, reflects the changing nature of people in the Third Age in contemporary Western society. It has already been pointed out that Bashevis Singer deals with this theme in his stories. This emphasis may be related to the fact that he is Jewish and is not writing in the Western Christian tradition, which has perpetuated certain assumptions about the elderly. Another modern author in the Jewish tradition who writes realistically about old people is Saul Bellow. In his *Mr Sammler's Planet* he makes Artur Sammler, aged seventy-two, the central character and brings out very effectively the attempt of the young to deny sexuality to the old.[9] When Mr Sammler gives a lecture to a group of students, one of them expresses himself thus, wishfully attributing sexual impotence to the elderly man and using it as a general criticism of his value: 'Orwell was a fink. He was a sick counterrevolutionary. It's good he died when he did. And what you are saying is shit . . . Why do you listen to this effete old shit? What has he got to tell you? His balls are dry. He's dead. He can't come.'

Outside the Christian tradition, it is worth looking at Japanese writers. In a review of literature, Mary Sohngen lists eighty-seven novels published between 1950 and 1975 in America or the UK that are written from the perspective of a protagonist over the age of sixty.[10] She comments that among these novels written 'During this period when sexual frankness was an accepted element in fiction, only a few include the sexual activity – or the sexual fantasies

– of the protagonist.' There are, in fact, seven novels in this category and two of them are translations from the Japanese.

In the Japanese novel *The Twilight Years* by Sawako Arioshi there is a curious twist at the end.[11] There is an unwanted old grandfather, Shigezo, a very difficult and selfish old man who lives with his son and his daughter-in-law Akiko. This woman and the old man are the principal characters in the novel. It is upon her that the chief burden of looking after him falls, as well as being exploited by her husband and other members of the family. She openly discusses how they might get rid of the old man, for Shigezo has always been an egocentric and querulous man and he is even worse in his frustrated old age. However, Akiko just has to put up with him, as she puts up with the traditionally boorish treatment from her husband. Towards the end of the book, however, a very curious situation develops. Shigezo's personality appears to change for the better and in Akiko's presence an unsuspected masculine charm and sensitivity emerges. It is suggested that he is falling in love with his daughter-in-law. On her part this overworked and emotionally neglected housewife responds to the horrid old devil and a curiously tender relationship, although not an overtly sexual one, develops between them. The author appears to be trying to tell us that the old are sometimes horrible, selfish old monsters only because the society in which they live denies them the warmth of tender and erotically toned love.

A further Japanese novel in this genre that should be mentioned is Junichiro Tanizaki's *Diary of a Mad Old Man*, in which Utsugi, seventy-seven years old, has a curious erotic fixation on women's feet.[12] He falls in love with his daughter-in-law but is ashamed to declare his love and is frustrated in his sexuality. Consequently he becomes more and more kinky in his preoccupation with the woman's feet. He rightly recognizes, however, that his sexuality is an expression of his desire for life and this keeps him from sinking into apathy and senility.

If we return to the literature of the West, one American commentator has observed, 'Old age in modern American literature is
not the stuff of tragedy. A truly tragic hero must have strength and
dignity and purpose. But old age in twentieth-century fiction has
been denied all of these qualities. When old age appears at all in literary work it is apt to be not tragic, but pathetic. The central theme
is the weakness and dependency of old age.'[13]

But there has been almost a revolution in modern fiction.
Writers in the Western Christian tradition are now recognizing that
older people do have dignity and purpose and, indeed, erotic needs,
although the world of fiction and the world of reality are still far
apart. A quite remarkable exception to the writers in the Christian
tradition is Graham Greene who, after a series of gloomy novels in
which the Roman Catholic point of view was strongly stressed, went
into a period of depression during which he wrote nothing and then
recovered to produce a hilarious novel, *Travels with My Aunt*.[14] This
is the tale of a woman in her seventies who, after a lifetime of affairs
and prostitution, retains her sexual appetite unabated. As part of
her generally joyous lifestyle she continues to take new lovers and
ends up happily with one of her old lovers who is even older than
she but who shares her immense sexual charm, joy of life and
contempt for conventional morality. What happened to Graham
Greene in his personal life that caused this volte-face is not
known.

We have had one or two black comedies dealing with the horrors
of old people and their continuing loves and jealousies in post-war
society, such as Muriel Spark's *Memento Mori* and Kingsley Amis's
Ending Up and *The Old Devils*, but the erotic theme in literature
about old people is scarce.[15, 17, 18] Among the signs of a more positive approach that have been developing in the post-war years is the
work of Eudora Welty. Her 'Old Mr Marblehall' portrays an old man
who, regarded by his neighbours as having one foot in the grave,
married for the first time at the age of sixty and has one son born of

this elderly marriage.[18] But having built up the picture of an old man living sedately with his dull wife and solitary offspring, the story then reveals that Mr Marblehall has, in fact, two wives with a son by each and manages successfully to lead a double life, chuckling to himself about his own duplicity and maintained virility. He secretly manages to retain the habits of his randy youth, despite the stifling atmosphere of a life-denying society that would relegate him to the scrap-heap of the old and used-up if they could.

When V. S. Pritchett began to get quite old, he took to writing about older people, defying the stereotypes that society projects on them. He used the theme of the erotic impulse to remind people that they should try to live in the present and not in the past when they were much more physically vigorous. He has his character Mr Dawson, who in *The Spree* is aged seventy and a widower, say, 'I must not fall into that trap: old people live in the past. And I am not old! Old I am not!'[19] Mr Dawson meets a widow and at first he regards her simply in terms of the conventional 'old woman', noting the signs of age on her face. He later realizes that his real need is 'not for a face or even a voice or even for love, but for a body'. The idea that some people of this age who are deprived need sex more than companionship or love as an immediate concern may seem shocking to those in our society who are conditioned to accept the Darby and Joan stereotype of elderly people, as in Robert Burns's poem:

> John Anderson my jo, John,
> We clamb the hill taegither;
> And monie a canty day, John,
> We've had wi' ane anither:
> Now we maun totter down, John,
> But hand in hand we'll go,
> And sleep taegither at the foot,
> John Anderson my jo.[21]

What many people do not realize, however, is that this poem is a bowdlerized version of a bawdy traditional song that was published in a collection of verses that became sufficiently well known after Burns's death, to be published about 1800 under the title of *Merry Muses of Caledonia.*[22] In it the elderly wife complains of the growing sexual incapacity of her husband John Anderson:

> John Anderson my jo, John
> When first that ye began, John,
> Ye had as good a tail-tree,
> As ony ither man;
> But now it's waxen wan, John,
> And wrinkles to and fro;
> I've twa gae-ups for ae gae-down,
> John Anderson my jo.

The verses go on to relate how she is as good as ever and is at his disposal any time he likes, despite his inadequate 'tail-tree'. Commenting on these verses, James Kinsley approves of Burns's bowdlerized version since it 'alters the tone from the licentious complaint to affection, and out of the same air he makes a new song for old age in which passion has been changed to simple companionship'.[23]

The old bawdy song is of interest in that it shows that among common people it was well known in earlier times that a woman's sexual appetite was generally maintained in old age while a man's capacity was subject to decline. Strangely, sex researchers in the twentieth century such as Havelock Ellis and Alfred Kinsey and his colleagues appear to have been unaware of this very simple fact.

Of course old people want love, companionship and secure relationships, but so do people of all ages. The very young may play around for a while, but their sexual experimentation normally leads to genuine love relationships of some permanence. There is no reason at all why people in later life who find themselves single should be any different, except that they have often experimented in their younger years and are more aware of what they want. Men are less likely late in life to have the compulsive need to prove themselves through sexual adventures, but people may wonder whether some of them are seeking sex to prove to themselves that they are not over the hill. Well, that may be true of certain cases for both sexes, but if so it is better that they should try to keep the life force alive and, rather than following the model advanced by Robert Burns, take heed of Dylan Thomas:

> Do not go gentle into that good night,
> Old age should burn and rave at close of day;
> Rage, rage against the dying of the light.[23]

The theme of the erotic impulse as a force that keeps older people living vitally is expressed by an increasing number of modern writers. Bernard Malamud tries to make us see that at any age the allure of physical attractiveness is a potent force for making life meaningful and vigorous, although sometimes leading to frustration and sorrow. In Part 2 of this book the real-life account of Mario, the artist, is told by his ex-lover. He had a new lease of ebullient and creative life in his old age by virtue of his living with her, even though in the end his dissolute way of life brought it to an end. Malamud's story 'In Retirement' concerns Dr Morris, a widower aged sixty-six, who tries to combat his loneliness by turning to the study of classical Greek.[25] However, his repressed sexuality is awakened by finding an open letter addressed to his neighbour, an attractive young woman who is apparently sexually promiscuous. In his fantasy he pictures her in bed with her various lovers, engaged in various sexual acts. 'Once she lay alone, erotically naked in bed, her maroon cloth purse drawn close to her nude body.' He dwells obsessively on this image.

Dr Morris becomes more and more engrossed with this young woman, his desire invigorating him in a way that he has not experienced for years, but in spite of his better judgement he becomes more and more irrational. Finally he steals an unopened letter addressed to her and this inflames his passion still further. He convinces himself that forming some kind of relationship with her might be possible, so he writes to her suggesting that she comes over and spends an evening with him. He then has the humiliating experience of actually seeing her laugh as she tears up his letter. This is, of course, a pathetic ending to the story but, in contrast to earlier literature, it is not told in mockery of the man, as in Chaucer's tale of January and May. Rather, it is an acknowledgement of the realities of life: that the old no less than the young can experience precisely the same frustrations and misfortunes in love and that they need not lose their dignity. This is exemplified in Part 2 in Tina's account.

John Cheever's novel *The World of Apples* also deals with the theme of the erotic impulse in later life serving to reinvigorate a man but in a rather different way.[26] The story deals with Asa Bascomb, an American poet of some fame now living in an Italian village at the age of eighty-two. He is more or less reconciled to being an old man living in the past and dwelling on his previous achievements when a small incident reawakens sexual feelings that he has not experienced for many years and brings him into contact with the present. When walking in the woods he comes across a couple making love and, to his surprise, the image of the man's back and his copulatory activity begins to haunt him. This animal image 'seemed to have more zeal and meaning than his celebrated search for truth'. He begins to write a new sort of poetry, not the high-minded material of the past but earthy and salacious verses, revelling in sheer eroticism. He is ashamed of this work and destroys it, yet it leads him to read and appreciate the celebration of joyous sexuality in the works of Petronius and Juvenal and to a kind of rebirth of experience in his old age. To rid himself of his crude obsession with the scene he witnessed in the woods, he seeks to perform some cleansing rite and eventually achieves it by leaping naked into a waterfall, which for him is a particularly meaningful ritual. Although he regrets the interlude of his 'bestial' obsession with sex, having overcome it he realizes that it has changed his life for the good and was a means of bringing him into the present and asserting his will to live.

Celeste Loughman, in reviewing this new trend in modern literature, writes:

> In their most limited sense, these stories extend to the elderly the liberal sexual attitudes which other segments of the population have been experiencing. More than that, they challenge long-standing myths which have become codified into rigid social norms that have effectively severed old age from other stages of life. As behavioural science confirms, the persistence of the sexual impulse gives evidence that life is a continuum and that behaviour tolerated in the young should not be censured in the old.[27]

The above was written in 1983 and since then the liberalizing trend has continued. The theme of love and eroticism is no longer treated as the exclusive preserve of the young and no longer must all characters after middle age be regarded as sexless or morbidly inclined characters on the periphery of normal life, often portrayed as objects of derision. Several more recent novels exemplify this. In Louis de Bernières's novel *Captain Corelli's Mandolin* the lovers Antonio Corelli and Pelagia Iannis are separated for a long number of years after the war when he goes back to Italy. They grow old in their separation, but eventually Antonio manages to get back to Greece and finds Pelagia again, a grey old woman, and tells her that he has never married:

> 'Me? No. As I said, I was very bitter for years and years. I was horrible to everyone, especially to women, and then music took off

and I was all over the world. I had to leave the fire brigade. And anyway, you were always my Beatrice. My Laura. I thought, who wants second best? Who wants to be with someone, dreaming of someone else?'

'Antonio Corelli, I can see that you still tell lies with your silver tongue. And how can you bear to look on me now? I'm an old woman. And when you look at me I don't like it, because I remember what I was. I feel ashamed to be so old and ugly . . .'

He put his hand on hers and squeezed it gently and said, 'Don't worry. I'm with you for only a little while and it's still Pelagia. Pelagia with a bad temper, but still Pelagia.' [28]

But Antonio did not go away and the book ends with him taking her as a pillion rider on a motorcycle where she is glad of the excuse to cling closely to him, two old lovers riding towards their future life together.

That we are now in an era of fiction such as never existed before is exemplified in another novel by the following description of a love scene which begins a joyous honeymoon of two enraptured lovers:

Then he looked at her and saw her naked to her waist, just as he had imagined her. Her shoulders were wrinkled, her breasts sagged, her ribs were covered by a flabby skin as pale and cold as a frog's. She covered her chest with the blouse she had just taken off and she turned out the light. Then he sat up and began to undress in the darkness, throwing everything at her that he took off, while she tossed it back, dying of laughter. [29]

Thus begins the long-delayed consummation of the love between Firmina and Florentino in Gabriel García Márquez's novel *Love in the Time of Cholera*.[28] In no age other than the present could a novelist have written such a realistic description of the beginning of a delightful and erotic honeymoon between the heroine and hero of his novel at last united in their old age. It is a defiance of Father Time such as is celebrated in Shakespeare's sonnet:

> Love's not Time's fool, though rosy lips and cheeks
> Within his bending sickle's compass come;
> Love alters not with his brief hours and weeks,
> But bears it out even to the edge of doom. [30]

CHAPTER 3

Popular media images

Television

In the 1970s various studies were conducted in the USA and the UK which showed that older people were almost invisible on television. When they did appear in programmes it was either in the role of old dears mouthing platitudes in smaller roles or horrible figures of fun acting as foils for the main characters, whose young lives and loves were the predominant focus of interest. While it was possible to show older characters living together as Darby and Joan, or in comic bickering relationships, it was unheard of to show them forming new love relationships in later life.

Pressure was brought to bear on television companies in the USA by groups like the Gray Panthers, who pointed out that people over the age of sixty did exist in society and that their lives were as important as those of younger people.

As a result of their lobbying, changes began to occur in the programmes for the better, showing that it pays to make a fuss. Of course, commercial broadcasting companies are sensitive to complaints made by consumers of the products they advertise. The fact that many older people these days have disposable income – in contrast to the self-denying parsimony of the elderly in former times – made advertisers aware of an important market for their products and services.

In 1983 a study was carried out by the Research Committee of the University of the Third Age in Cambridge into the image of the elderly on television.[1] The committee decided to monitor one week's television broadcasting: the output of all four channels over the period, taking BBC 1 and Channel 4 during the first week and ITV and BBC 2 during the second.

The research employed fourteen monitors, ten of whom were over the age of sixty and all of whom were members of the local branch of the University of the Third Age, which has no actual age limits for membership. It is worth noting that when the results were analysed it was found that there was no significant difference between the older and younger monitors regarding the fairness or unfairness of the presentation of older characters. The monitors were expected to identify those characters who were 'elderly persons' appearing to be sixty years of age or older. Since many of them appeared on the screen for very short periods of time, seconds rather than minutes, appraisals had to be made very rapidly. It is possible therefore that the same characters might be appraised differently by various monitors but, as nearly five hundred programmes were monitored, such error was probably evened out.

All types of programme had instances of elderly people being absent; this was particularly noticeable in plays, serials, soap operas, action/adventure programmes, sitcoms, schools and education programmes, feature films and cartoons and children's programmes. Older people appeared more frequently in programmes concerned with the news, current affairs and documentaries. This was to be expected, as many prominent figures in the world are over sixty.

As nearly one-fifth of the population of the UK can now be classed as elderly, a fair presentation of group or crowd scenes would naturally reflect them roughly in this proportion, or perhaps a little less, as older people tend to go out publicly less often. In fact, where groups of people were shown, only about 10 to 15 per cent of people were recognizable as elderly. One striking feature of this inquiry relates to the sex of the older people shown. Although there are a lot more women among the elderly population, they were grossly under-represented in television programmes and they were seldom in central roles. As for the class structure, over four-fifths of those appearing belonged to the managerial and professional classes. This bias was less pronounced in fictional programmes, where older working-class women had some significant role in popular soap operas such as *Coronation Street*. Taking into account both the sex and class distortions of the general presentations, in summarizing their findings the authors of the research reported:

> The result can only be called a caricature of the real social world of the British elderly . . . an important reason why the elderly as we know them are negligible in television appearance is because the successful elderly people who do figure there are not regarded as elderly in society. Thus, even when they are themselves biologically elderly, politicians and leaders do not represent the elderly as a social category.[2]

The main purpose of this study was, of course, to investigate how commonly older people were represented on television relative to their actual frequency in the population and how fair this representation was. But it is of interest to note how the theme of love in later life was dealt with by programme-makers in 1983. The short answer is that it was almost wholly ignored.

An attempt was made to rate the elderly shown in the programmes on fifteen characteristics, such as 'wise/foolish', 'active/passive' and 'fit/infirm'. The one characteristic that proved to be very obviously different from the others was 'sexually active/inactive', because it simply did not apply in most cases and so was not rateable. This was true even bearing in mind that it was not normal elderly people who were shown on television so often as rich and influential celebrities who were overwhelmingly male. For instance, compare the two ratings in Figure 1.

Figure 1. Active vs passive characteristics
of older people on television (one week in 1983)

Age	No. of rateable appearances	Rating	
		Active	Passive
60s	517	407	110
70s	170	134	36
80s	22	13	9
		Sexually active	Inactive
60s	34	28	6
70s	10	6	4
80s	3	2	1

It is obvious from these figures that the question of whether a character was rateable on his or her sexual activity was seldom possible because the theme hardly applied to older characters.

The authors of the report commented:

These results tend to confirm those already reported . . . They also bear out the existence of some of the ill-informed and sometimes rather prejudiced attitudes already known to the students of the social life of elderly people, exaggerating the incomes of the elderly, for example, and playing down the possibility of their having to be judged at all on their sexual activity.[3]

Things have improved on television over the past ten years or so, partly owing to agitation from pressure groups but also because many older people who are relatively affluent have changed in their attitude to their accumulated wealth. They are no longer prepared to hoard money for the sake of their descendants. Knowing that they cannot take it with them when they die, they are beginning to spend it in order to live more comfortable lives, thus forming an important new market. Purchasing power counts with television advertisers and the 'grey pound' is just one of the factors that has influenced them to make some attempt to woo the older viewer.

Thus British viewers now have programmes such as *Tea and Sympathy*, where three sets of lovers appear: young, middle-aged and elderly. Other programmes include *Waiting for God*, where a romance is in progress between two of the residents of an old people's home and their amorous antics are sympathetically depicted, and *One Foot in the Grave*, where the sexual misadventures of an elderly couple are sometimes portrayed with almost Rabelaisian gusto. In contrast with the tradition of making love in old age the subject of mockery, it is now treated with respect even in comedy programmes. On *Blind Date*, a dating show that culminates in a man and a woman, previously strangers, going away on holiday together, elderly people have been included among the participants. The old taboos have been broken and older people are now beginning to be treated like everyone else.

Another survey of television programmes was conducted by Eric Midwinter on behalf of the Centre for Policy on Ageing in 1990.[4] Dr Midwinter approached a number of prominent television producers, features controllers, directors of programmes, editors of newspapers and well-known journalists, asking them to respond to the question: 'Given that there are between thirteen and fourteen million older people in the UK, how do you feel about the way they are presented in the press and on television

and radio, perhaps with special reference to your own interests?'
He pointed out that two issues had been widely canvassed.

One is that the image of older people in the media is negative and
that they are represented in a condescending, unduly comical, or
problem-oriented manner with insufficient coverage of the more
positive aspects of older age. The other is that, put simply, old age
is practically invisible in the press and on the media and, compared
with total numbers, old people are vastly under-represented in
newspapers and on radio and television.

Regarding television, a number of the respondents admitted
that there were problems and made remarks such as: 'In attempt-
ing to get publicity for *Primetime* I find that the national newspapers as a matter of policy do find the elderly "not sexy".
Following the campaigns against sexism and racism, there must
now be one against ageism.' Others blamed fundamental features
of modern society: 'Until society finds new, useful roles for the
elderly, most of the popular media will be tempted to look at them
through the same old patronizing spectacles.' There were also
those connected with television, who tended to question whether
the criticisms were entirely justified: 'Of course, some older people
are treated as problems or as comical – as are those of other age
groups – but the majority are taken seriously and portrayed fairly.
Indeed the image is often of older people having authority, particularly in journalistic programmes.'

It is difficult to compare the 1990 research with that of the
Cambridge team in 1983 because the two surveys were conducted
in a very different manner. The former produced a great deal of
opinion from within the television world, anxious to justify what
it was doing in the face of problems that were not of its making.
Midwinter makes the point that in all forms of media there is a gap
between what the viewers or other recipients perceive and reality,

and he refers to television as the most vivid example of this gap. Referring to the programme *Last of the Summer Wine* he writes:

> There is no avoiding the fact that the pursuit of the older woman, Norah Batty, right down to the last erotic tug of her wrinkled stockings, by the energetic, disreputable Compo is a classic confrontation of the unattractive older woman and the dirty old man. This is in part a class-based cameo, but it does underline the amalgam of hilarity and revulsion with which sexuality in older age is regarded.

If this is indeed so, I would say that it is about time the programme in question was purged of such offensive material. When black people appear on television they are no longer represented as stupid, slovenly, lazy and irredeemably comic as was the case in many old films of the 1920s. It seems regrettable that in the single case of a man showing erotic interest in a woman in this programme he should be portrayed as a 'dirty old man' and she as remarkably unattractive.

Press images

In contrast to presentations on television the printed media offers a very wide spectrum of representations of elderly people, ranging from the *Sun* to the *Independent* and from *Hello* to the *Times Literary Supplement*. When Eric Midwinter wrote to various editors and journalists on behalf of the Centre for Policy on Ageing, the replies he published were received from newspapers such as *The Times*, the *Guardian*, the *Independent* and sundry well-known and responsible journalists. Their opinions are no doubt very valuable in gaining an assessment of how it is acceptable for intelligent papers to strike a balance between newsworthiness and the educational value of presenting 'the elderly' to the public. Midwinter writes:

The balance of the discussion might be to suggest that, yes, there are some difficulties with the position of older people in the press and media but, no, it is not a problem of epic proportions and, be careful, the remedy might be as bad as the sickness. Overriding the comments as such is the encouraging sense of journalists and broadcasters prepared to give the question credence as a significant issue, and, from their various professional standpoints, to think with care about it.

It is a complicated issue and there is nothing to be gained from pontificating simplistically. It has to be set against the changing definition of older age and the resultant gap between traditional and avant-garde delineations. With this in mind and encouraged by the good sense of the views expressed by the journalists and broadcasters who have generously helped with this report, we should now take a closer look at how the definition of older age is changing and the new realities that need to be addressed.[5]

I suggest that if the editors of such newspapers as the *News of the World*, the *Sun* and the *Mirror* (all with much larger circulations than the three mentioned above) had given their views on how the image of elderly people should be presented, we would have got a rather different set of opinions. No doubt the quality papers influence people who are individually more powerful in society, but, taking our society as a whole, it is probably the papers with mass readership that are the more important in forming and maintaining opinions about older people. The issues that were referred to in the replies received and those discussed were concerned with matters such as frequency of mention of older people, the relevance of referring to their age, the lack of adequate comment on their achievements, the use of patronizing words such as 'Granny' and the too-frequent representation of older people in the role of dependent and victim.

This is perfectly understandable in view of the wording of the questions asked; what was not mentioned was the rarity of regarding older people as generally having a love life like most other people in society. People's emotional and erotic needs are quite frequently the subject of comment in the printed media, unless they are considered 'elderly'. There are a few outstanding exceptions: when they are famous in some way, as in the marriage of Peregrine Worsthorne: 'Lucy and Peregrine are clearly dotty about each other. Their romance has all the impetuously abandoned madness of youth.'[6] Again, if there is a gross discrepancy between the ages of the partners one get headlines such as: 'Rural dean of seventy marries blonde model of twenty', and if both partners are quite exceptionally aged: 'Great-granddad of ninety-nine and his bride of one hundred'.

The press puts the association between age and sex in a special category. In 1995 I gave a lecture on sexual relations in later life to a learned society. To my amazement it provoked countrywide press comment, much of it wildly inaccurate. In the course of my lecture I naturally drew attention to the fact that in the older decades of life there is growing numerical excess of women as they live longer than men, and the natural result of this was likely to be an increasing number of same-sex partnerships between women. This provoked headlines such as, 'Lesbo love boom – girls are grabbin' the girls – guys!' (*Daily Sport*), 'Have a gay old time!' (*Evening Gazette*), 'Lack of older men turns grey women gay' (*Evening Leader*), 'Sex life begins at 50' (*Daily Mirror*), 'On your dyke!' (*Tonight*). I did not bother to write to these and similar papers complaining of the gross misrepresentation of my lecture; there were too many of them and they would simply have contrived to blow up the whole thing into a glorious field-day of mockery and salaciousness. However, I was moved to complain to the editors of the *Daily Telegraph* and the *Independent on Sunday* for having misrepresented my lecture so badly and they printed my letters of protest. I found it specially disturbing that the journalist writing in the latter paper had not bothered to read the press release about my lecture but relied entirely on the inaccurate report published in the former paper, thus misrepresenting it still further.

Finally, consider the following news item which appeared in the *News of the World:*

> Police had to break up a street fight between two love rivals aged 94 and 87. The grappling granddads came to blows over an eighty-seven-year-old woman. Jilted James Young, 94, flew into a rage when he found his girlfriend of 12 years was seeing another pensioner. Mr Young of Southwark, south London, said, 'I won't see her any more.'[7]

Fights between men over women are so common that they are simply ignored by the media. The only reason for the paper printing this event was the age of the protagonists. Are the readers supposed to admire the sustained vigour of these people or are they supposed to hoot with laughter at the perceived ridiculousness of the whole affair? It seems that as far as the printed media are concerned they have not moved far from Chaucer's bawdy jesting about love expressed by people who are perceived as 'old' if they have the misfortune not to be in some way famous. It is interesting that the changes that are beginning to take place in television have affected the press so little.

Treatment of older people's sex lives in popular humour

Jokes are a barometer of how people feel about things, hence the popularity of sex jokes and lavatory humour in the aftermath of Victorian prudery and of black political jokes in repressive regimes. There have been a number of studies of how the perceived nastiness of growing old and the ridiculousness of older people aspiring to a sex life is reflected in popular humour. One review of jokes about old people revealed that over half of them showed a highly negative attitude and that ageing women were the especial butt of aggressive humour. Another study compared jokes concerning the elderly with those involving children and found that whereas most of the jokes about children were appreciative, viewing them in a positive if 'quaint' light, most of the jokes about old people were derogatory, ridiculing them because they were supposed to get more stupid as they aged and mocking their physical decay and, in particular, the decline of their sexual powers. A few jokes were more complex, however, turning upon those who denigrate the elderly because their turn to be ridiculous would arise in the course of time. A few jokes affirmed that some old people have a lot more life in them than is generally supposed, old men being shown as being absurd whatever they do, seen either as sexless wrecks or oversexed lechers. The following joke illustrates the latter characteristic:

> An old man who had just married a girl of twenty went to his doctor for advice because he wanted to keep his young bride happy so that she would remain kind and patient with him and he might beget an heir. The doctor advised him to get a young female companion for his wife to live in their home, and so he imported an au pair girl. Three months later the doctor saw the old fellow and asked him, 'How's your wife?'
>
> 'Fine! She's pregnant.'
>
> 'So the au pair girl kept her happy?'
>
> 'Yes, and she's pregnant too.' [8]

Among the various theories offered about the meaning and function of jokes there are two specially worth considering: the disparagement theory and the incongruity model. It is easy to interpret jokes about old people in terms of disparagement theory but, unlike racist and sexist jokes, the younger people who make them know that they themselves will eventually be joining the group that is the butt of their humour. There is no way in which they can avoid taking on all the alleged characteristics of the stigmatized group except by dying young.

In the incongruity model, there is a necessary paradox to be perceived: that the crowing young man taking pride in his strength and virility will one day have to accept the decline that is in store for him and if he does continue to show erotic interest he will be called 'a dirty old man'. This is the riddle of the Sphinx that was posed to Oedipus: he who walks on two legs at noon will walk on three in the evening; that is, he will have to use a walking stick when he's old. Again, if the old manage to retain their vigour and sexual potency, the envious young would like to think of them as paying for it in some other way and therefore remaining a figure of mockery, as in the following joke:

An old man skilfully defeated a group of much younger men at a gymnasium in a variety of athletic sports. 'You must be at least seventy years old,' said one of the young men admiringly, 'yet you beat us at everything. Are you that good at everything?'

'Not at all,' said the old man. 'I'm not the man I used to be. For instance, when I went to bed last night I did my duty by my wife and then in the morning I did it again. I then got up and had a shower, but when I came back to the bedroom I repeated the whole performance. You see, my memory is going.' [9]

That ageist jokes are particularly derogatory of women is an example of the tragedy of the macho male's approach to sex: the knowledge that whoever he loves for her blooming, youthful charm will be taken from him inevitably when she changes with age. She will, in fact, be like his mother-in-law. There is, of course, the traditional mother-in-law joke: this aged female figure, ugly, stupid and domineering, has no counterpart in a father-in-law figure.

A. I've formed quite an attachment for my mother-in-law.

B. How strange!

A. Yes, it fits over her mouth.

The above is a mild joke about mothers-in-law and refers to the common belief that such women talk too much and give unwanted advice to their married children, but there is a large anthology of obscene, demotic jokes of an aggressive nature directed against the figure of the wife's (not the husband's) mother, which address the special tension that exists between many men and such older women who occupy this unique role in their lives.

The connection between mothers-in-law and attitudes of younger men to the sexual lives of older people may not be immediately apparent, but, according to anthropologists, it is a problem that is found worldwide in many different cultures. The older woman represents what the young wife will become in the course of years when time, the perceived enemy of love, will have turned her into an old woman. Christopher Wilson in his scholarly book *Jokes: Form, Content, Use and Function* cites the following joke to illustrate the complexity of the relations between the different generations with regard to their attitudes to one another's sexual expression:

A liberal father, anxious that his sixteen-year-old son should be painlessly initiated into the mysteries of sex, gives the boy £20 and dispatches him in pursuit of a prostitute. Later the son returns and proudly tells his father that he has been doubly successful, losing his virginity while saving the £20.

'I told Granny where I was going,' explained the boy, 'and she said she'd do it for free.'

'What,' screamed the father, 'you screwed my mother?'

'Why not?' asked the son. 'You screwed mine.' [10]

Freudians might tell us that this joke refers to the fact that sons never quite forgive their fathers for what they have done to their mothers. Some people will find the joke very distasteful and indeed disturbing, for Dr Wilson tells us that in various cultures all over the world it is a common clownish jest for men to pretend that they wish to sleep with their grandmothers. The attitude of young and middle-aged children towards their parents' forming new sexual relationships in later life will be discussed in Chapter 4.

Freud's theory of the function of humour was that it allows us to express in the guise of frivolity deep-seated impulses of hostility and sexual aggression. All those who have seriously examined the content of jokes to ascertain their meaning have found that a large percentage of them are directed against older women. As women age they frustrate men sexually by losing those characteristics which younger men find specially attractive. The following joke expresses this form of humour:

> A pretty little girl went to a draper's shop and asked for some cloth to make a dress for her doll. The young man there selected a remnant and handed it to the girl.
>
> 'How much is it?' she asked.
>
> 'Just one kiss,' the man replied.
>
> 'All right,' said the girl as she turned to go. 'Grandma said to tell you that she would pay you when she came by tomorrow.'[11]

Here it is assumed that Grandma will be, as a matter of course, an unprepossessing figure whom no man would wish to kiss.

Representations in birthday cards

Birthday cards are particularly significant as they remind people of the passing years and of the spectre of old age that looms ahead. Those designed to be sent to older relatives are typically sentimental and cheerful, reassuring the recipients that they do not look their age. It is those designed to be sent to contemporaries that frequently contain crude jokes of a sexual nature about the coming of old age with all its supposed horrors, especially the loss of physical attractiveness and potency. Such cards usually display an elderly person, generally a woman, who is not only obviously aged but ugly as well. I have one which displays such a grim figure with the caption 'Getting old is fun.' Inside the card is the statement 'Me – I'd rather have a cute bum', thus contrasting the sexual attractiveness of a young woman with the perceived awfulness and asexuality of the old.

Such cards, like all ageist jokes, display just what racist and sexist jokes display: fear. The 'Rastus' jokes against black men (which used to be common before racism became a sensitive issue) displayed the dominant white man's fear that those he exploited would rise up against him. Similarly, sexist jokes against women reveal the anxiety that the exploited female will emancipate herself from male dominance. Ageist jokes show two sorts of fear: first, fear that old people will no longer accept their status of pathetic old sexless beings, fit only to poke the fire and look after the grandchildren, but defy the age-old conventions and adopt lifestyles that the young consider to be their prerogative; second, there is the fear of the fate looming ahead of the young themselves.

How do older people react to ageist cards and demotic humour in general that pillories them as figures to be mocked, particularly with respect to their sex life or its absence? A little while ago I came across two shops selling cards depicting elderly people, mostly women, who were quite grotesque in their ugliness, some of them bearing messages inside that verged on the obscene. Had such cards depicted people of an ethnic minority with their racial characteristics grotesquely exaggerated and accompanied by jeering messages they would have been liable to criminal prosecution. There are laws against racism but none against ageism. One of the shops, a well-known stationers, agreed to withdraw the cards after

71

my protest to their head office. The owner of the other shop adamantly refused to withdraw them as he said they were very profitable.

I bought a number of these cards and showed them to a group of older women who were attending a class I was running. To my surprise a number of the women roared with laughter at them and one asked me where she might obtain them. This is an interesting defensive reaction that has been developed by many people in later life who have had to come to terms with the prevailing stereotypes of 'the old', similar to that of Jewish people who have had to contend with virulent anti-Semitism over the centuries. The Jews have developed a huge repertoire of anti-Semitic jokes that mock every aspect of their culture, religion and physical appearance. They have by this means, as it were, cauterized themselves against criticism and derision, for they can tell a better anti-Semitic joke than any gentile.

Possibly the 'new old', that is the rising generation who are coming into the Third Age with less acceptance of second-class citizenship, will not tolerate a public display of ageism any more than ethnic minorities are prepared to tolerate public expression of racism.

CHAPTER 4

New partnerships

While most of those concerned with the study of ageing are agreed that it is a very good thing for those rendered single in later life to form new partnerships, there are serious problems to be considered. From the point of view of many doctors, social workers and particularly those running residential and nursing homes for the elderly, it may be much more administratively convenient if single elderly people were resigned to a celibate life. When a fire is quietly smouldering, they may ask, why stoke it up into a blaze with all the attendant problems? We know that the sex drive does decline with age, particularly with men, so it might be better to encourage elderly people to remain as prim old ladies in lavender and lace and harmless old men whose greatest excitement is playing bowls, according to the traditional stereotype. Modern books such as the Greengrosses' *Living, Loving and Ageing* positively encourage them to seek sexual partners with all the hurly-burly involved, such as women badgering their doctors for hormone replacement therapy and men demanding treatment for failing potency.[1]

The people who have most to complain of about this modern tendency are those who run residential homes for the elderly, where not only is it most inconvenient to have residents snogging in odd corners, but there is understandable jealousy on the part of those who have not got partners. Such jealousy is often expressed in terms of strong moral disapproval and a quarrelsome atmosphere is created. Fortunately only about 3 per cent of the retired population live in such homes, so it is not a major social problem and bodies such as Age Concern, recognizing that there is now so strong a current of feeling in favour of the expression of sexuality in later life that it cannot and should not be checked, are taking active steps to educate care workers to deal with the issue sympathetically.

With regard to the supposed extra burden created for the medical and social services by the rejection of a celibate way of life by many now entering the Third Age, the following facts should be considered. It is true that quite a lot of elderly people are perfectly happy and healthy living completely sexless lives, but one thing that is becoming increasingly clear is that, as we age, we become more unalike, each individual developing in his or her unique way. Nearly 90 per cent of us marry at some time in our lifetime so it is evident that the statistical norm is to seek a partner of the opposite sex at some stage. Statistics also tell us that pairing off contributes to continued health in later life and to longevity. People living alone, especially men, do not live as long as those who have partners. This is generally attributed to the fact that those with partners have someone to look after them and restrain them from drinking too much, eating unwisely and generally going to seed. A well-known social scientist, E. M. Palmore, who has looked into this matter in great detail, differs from his colleagues in claiming that he has found that the longer life of married men is directly due not principally to the married state but to the degree of sexual satisfaction within marriage.[2]

Superficially it may appear that anything that causes people to live longer is imposing an extra burden on the medical and social services, but this is a fallacy. The ideal is for people to live in independence, vigour and health until the day they die and therefore not need medical and social services. Increased longevity depends on such continued health and some doctors have predicted that, in the future, we should have a decreased need for geriatric care accompanying a longer-lived population. It stands to reason that if older people are living in couples then they will be able to look after one another and not require the services of professional carers.

Economic problems in the family

The acquisition of a new partner in later life by a man or a woman sometimes raises serious problems in families, as occurred in the case of Gertrude and her husband (see Part 2). One obvious reason for middle-aged children to resent a bereaved or separated parent forming a new partnership is that the inheritance may be divided, the newcomer inheriting some or all of the family money on their parent's decease. There is even the possibility that an elderly father may beget more children if his new wife is of childbearing age and these will compete with the existing children. Where an economic conflict is involved, the children of the first marriage may convince themselves that their elderly parent is being exploited by a gold-digging floozy or a mercenary toyboy, whatever the real facts of the case. Armed with righteous indignation they may try to muster all the forces of the larger family to prevent the coming marriage, using whatever forms of emotional blackmail are available.

Thirty years ago Margaret Mead advanced an ingenious suggestion for a new form of marriage that would go some way to eliminate this kind of trouble in families.[3] She proposed that there should be two forms of marriage. One form should be purely contractual and carry no rights of inheritance, and this should be particularly suitable for men and women in later life who wish to live together and have their union officially recognized but who do not wish to cause the particular form of family conflicts that have been mentioned. Children of a former marriage might be happier if their mother or father formed a union that did not in any way threaten their right of inheritance. Mead's idea was that a marriage of this form could be contracted at any age, but if children resulted from the union it would then be automatically converted into the conventional form of marriage, which gives protection to the children and puts legal obligations and responsibilities on both partners.

Margaret Mead's idea of a new form of marriage had more relevance thirty years ago; now, when public attitudes have changed towards people living together unmarried, it is perhaps outmoded. However, some couples in later life still wish to have their union regularized by the traditional form of marriage and, if that is the case, they may wish to make special legal arrangements about the inheritance of property to obviate any future family discord. Premarital legal planning may therefore be advisable and they might be well advised to seek the advice of a solicitor regarding the formation of trusts and so on and inform the existing beneficiaries of their will about what they are doing. These arrangements may allay the fears of children and other family members who might have an interest in the estate.

It is by no means uncommon nowadays for older people who fall in love and form a permanent relationship that is recognized by all their friends and relatives not only to dispense with marriage but to continue to live in separate abodes and to keep their financial arrangements entirely separate. This is partly the result of the feminist movement, which has stressed the need for women's autonomy. An older woman, rendered single by bereavement or divorce and having brought up a family and looked after a husband in the traditional role, may feel when she enters the Third Age that she wishes to put all that behind her and live a free and independent life just as she did as a young woman before she married, while still enjoying a love life and all that goes with it with a lover. She may feel that if she moves in to live with her lover she will revert to her previous pattern of behaviour, which involved many domestic chores and responsibilities. If her children and his are the sort of people who worry about inheritance, such an arrangement may go some way to allaying their fears for the future.

In discussing economic problems which may cause family conflict we should also consider what may be called the 'King Lear syndrome'. It will be remembered that in Shakespeare's play the old king decided to hand over his kingdom to his three daughters and trusted them to see that he lived out his old age in a comfortable and honoured retirement. Once two of them (having ousted the third sister from favour) had gained control of his property and power, they proceeded steadily to impoverish the old man and to reduce him to madness by their ingratitude. Elderly parents should learn wisdom from this play.

Although children may profess proper love and duty towards their aged parents when the latter hold the purse-strings, when an inheritance is at stake their attitudes may change radically. It is sometimes the case that a son-in-law or daughter-in-law will constantly ask 'When is the old man going to pop off?' and perhaps nag the spouse into a line of conduct foreign to his or her natural feelings. It is possible to make a deed of family settlement, whereby inheritance tax is obviated by the parents making over the family estate to future inheritors. In such a case they may be 'lent' the capital so that they may benefit from the interest during their lifetime. Such arrangements may involve complex legal provisos and depend on a degree of trust within the families and the presumption that a parent will not remarry or take on additional financial commitments in later life. Perhaps a proper degree of trust may exist at the time such an arrangement is made, but in these uncertain times a middle-aged child may acquire a new spouse who may set to work like Goneril and Regan to deprive the aged parents or parent of their moral rights. It would seem better for those in later life not to assume that because of their age they should retire from retaining full responsibility for their affairs.

Emotional problems caused by a new relationship
Quite apart from economic problems that can follow from a single parent acquiring a new partner in later life, there may be a serious

conflict owing to emotional problems. The most typical of these situations is where a son is involved in an unhappy marriage and strongly resents the remarriage of an elderly father or mother. In the case of his father it is simple jealousy. He asks himself, 'Why should the old man at his age be able to attract a new partner, whereas I am stuck with this awful wife of mine? I thought the old devil was past it!' This would also apply to a son who has never been able to find a satisfactory woman who would accept him or who has been divorced and made to feel unattractive. Sons can be equally resentful of their mothers remarrying or having a lover and here it is the jealousy that the Freudians have called 'Oedipal'. It is most graphically displayed in the Queen's bedchamber scene of *Hamlet*, where the eponymous hero tries to make his mother feel ashamed of going to bed with her second husband, Claudius, stating that a woman of her age should be past it:

> O shame! Where is thy blush? Rebellious hell,
> If thou canst mutine in a matron's bones
> To flaming youth, let virtue be as wax
> And melt in her own fire; proclaim no shame
> When the compulsive ardour gives the charge
> Since frost itself as actively doth burn,
> And reason panders will.
> . . .
> Nay but to live
> In the rank sweat of an enseamed bed
> Stewed in corruption, honeying and making love
> Over a nasty sty —[4]

One might think that Hamlet's words in describing his mother's love-making were over the top, but I have witnessed similar expressions of disgust by sons faced with their mother's remarriage. I was invited on to a television programme in the capacity of an expert commentator where they had gathered a large number of members of the public. The assembly was made up of parents who were contemplating, or had already contracted, marriages in later life and whose children were objecting for various reasons. Both sons and daughters were stating their objections and I noted that the most vigorous protests came from sons outraged at their mother's intentions, although daughters also objected, principally on the grounds that they thought that their fathers were being exploited by younger women. It was difficult to reason with these people because they expressed themselves in such emotional terms.

One of the arguments that frequently arose was that participants thought their bereaved parents were not showing sufficient respect to the deceased father or mother. One could have some sympathy with this feeling in cases where the death had occurred quite recently, but where the death had apparently occurred some years earlier it seemed likely that the objection was being used as a cover for less admirable motives.

I have known the case where a middle-aged son, on learning that his widowed father in his seventies had taken up with a perfectly respectable woman in her sixties, referred to her when speaking to friends as his father's 'fancy piece'. This son had rather an unhappy, childless marriage and since that time ten years ago he has not seen his father again. Butler and Lewis, who have extensive experience of the problems of older people, discuss the problem in their excellent book *Love and Sex After Sixty*, pointing out that it is entirely sensible for elderly parents to remarry if they can and that many children will welcome such an occurrence for practical reasons. They go on to say:

> For still other children the reactions are entirely emotional. The thought of a parent becoming involved with a new partner can provoke anxiety, threat, jealousy, anger or grief. They may be strongly inclined to offer unasked for advice and even to take over

if they feel that a parent is making a mistake. Coercion, threats and angry withdrawal are not uncommon.[5]

The authors point out that there are numerous reasons why some adult children act in such an irrational way. In some cases the parent may be partly at fault because the child has never become fully independent after he or she has grown up and the child has continued to use that parent to fulfil emotional needs that should have been met by their contemporaries. In such a case the child behaves in an unreasonable way that is not unlike that of a rejected and wounded lover. It seems absurd that a man of fifty should have such an intense relationship with his mother, but such cases are not uncommon. There is no easy solution to this sort of problem, but it is disastrous if the mother gives in to her son and gives up her lover, for by so doing she cements a totally abnormal sort of relationship. In abandoning her prospects of happiness she will harbour a grudge against the son and he may live to regret it. Perhaps in her frail old age she will feel that she has every right to impose on him without limit and for the rest of her life he will be prevented from finding a mate even if an opportunity occurs.

It is not only single men who remain over-dependent even in their fifties. Such dependency can continue even though a man is married and has children of his own, in which case his wife will have good cause to feel slighted if her mother-in-law, having sacrificed her own chance of independent happiness with a second husband, becomes an incubus on the family.

Where the children feel genuinely shocked that a widowed parent contemplates remarriage, because it is felt to be an insult to the idealized dear departed even after a number of years' bereavement, it generally means that they have not properly worked through their feelings over the death. Such feelings may even arise where there is a feeling of guilt, as when they believe that they did not treat their father properly when he was alive and now, although they may have no intellectual belief in the afterlife, they have a superstitious fear that his ghost may haunt them if offended. In the Shakespeare scene quoted above, the ghost of Hamlet's father is making his presence felt to Hamlet in the Queen's bedchamber and making Hamlet feel very guilty that he has failed to fulfil his duty to his late father by taking revenge on his mother's fickleness. Shakespeare was indeed a wise psychologist.

That children should find it almost impossible to accept the fact that their parents make love, like anyone else, is well known. The humorist Sam Levinson wrote, 'When I first found out how babies were made I couldn't believe it! To think that my mother and father would do such a thing! My father, maybe, but my mother never!' The fact that one's parents must have engaged in such behaviour at some time in the past must be believed, but when these parents are far past the age of making babies yet deliberately engaging in such behaviour – and with another partner – it may cause an emotional shock to middle-aged children, particularly when a son–mother relationship is involved.

It is not only quasi-incestuous relationships in the family that provoke resentment against a parent remarrying in later life. Common sense should tell us that there are a great number of reasons why children should feel thwarted by their parents, sometimes quite irrationally, for people who have made a mess of their lives like to have someone to blame. In other cases the children may have perfectly legitimate reasons for holding grievances against their parents. In more repressive days many parents thought it right severely to condemn and limit fairly harmless expressions of sexuality in children, just as they had been repressed by their own parents, still imbued with Victorian values. Now in more liberal days these adult children may look back on their own early childhood and teenage years and harbour a grudge against those who brought them up. Such grudges may lead to a wish to pay back those who have thwarted us in the past: 'She cruelly prevented me from rolling in the hay with Charlie and ruined a wonderful romance, so now I'm not prepared to countenance her making a fool of herself with that toyboy!'

Troubles arising from misinformation

Although most enlightened people nowadays realize that there is nothing abnormal about people in the later decades of life wanting a sex life, this knowledge is by no means universal. Some still believe that there is something pathological about a mother in her sixties taking a lover after some years of celibacy and think she must be in need of psychiatric treatment. More tolerance is generally shown towards elderly fathers if they remarry a younger partner, for a double standard is maintained towards the sex life of men and women. While he may be partly excused on the grounds that a younger woman will look after the old fellow, if he marries or takes a lover even older than himself the situation may be regarded with frank amazement by his children and indeed by many of his peers.

Now that so many people live a long time, it is not unusual for elderly parents to be looking after, or at least keeping in touch with, their own parents who are in their late eighties or nineties. Lovers in later life may therefore find themselves caught between the disapproval of two sets of relatives: middle-aged children motivated by economic and emotional feelings and very elderly parents who simply cannot understand why they are behaving in a manner which to them is bizarre: 'You always were a wild girl, Polly, but I think it's time you settled down now you're in your seventies. He's not the sort of man who'll marry you, my dear.'

While it may be almost impossible to educate some parents in their late eighties and nineties about the realities of love and sex in later life, an attempt can be made to talk to middle-aged children about the realities of the modern world and even to suggest books they should read. They may cling to the image of their parents being just 'Mum' and 'Dad' and not see them as individuals who have the same needs as everyone else. Parents, whatever their age, should insist that they be regarded in the same light as other people. In the 1960s there was a radical change in public attitudes to the sexuality of young and middle-aged people and it became quite respectable for couples to live together without being married if they so wished. In the 1970s a plethora of books was published dealing with factual matters regarding sex and the many possibilities of love-making, such as Alex Comfort's *The Joy of Sex*,[6] but these were directed mainly at the young. It was not until the 1980s that a number of serious books by reputable specialists in gerontology began to appear, mainly published in the USA, which made it clear that the abolition of the taboos which used to restrict the sex lives of the young should apply equally to elderly people.[7]

The exploitation of grandmothers

It is sad but true that women have greater problems in later life just because they are female and, despite the achievements of the feminist movement, they are still expected to carry responsibilities that are not demanded of men. A woman who has worked hard all her life and raised a family may expect to enjoy her leisure in her years of retirement, but her children may have other plans for her if she is a grandmother. Her domestic and child-minding skills may be called upon if her daughter wishes to buy her own leisure at the expense of her mother's. The idea of Mum, who has been living singly for some years, acquiring a new husband or lover may be very unwelcome news to a daughter who regards her own pursuits as more important than those of her mother. Previously she had perhaps regarded herself as doing a favour to her old mother by asking her to come and mind the children, cook some meals, clean the house and usefully occupy herself instead of living aimlessly as a widow.

It is true that most women take an active interest in the

upbringing of their grandchildren and in helping their middle-aged daughters in a practical way where normal affection exists in the family. There is an old and true saying:

> My son is my child till he gets him a wife,
> But my daughter's my child the whole of my life.

However, a woman who has reached the years of retirement may expect to enjoy a love relationship with a man as well as continuing to love her daughter and grandchildren and show an active interest in their welfare. Indeed, if she is enjoying an erotic relationship with someone, she is less likely to be jealous of her daughter for having an active sex life. A grandmother who is satisfied with her life is less likely to become the 'crabbed old witch' of folklore who interferes with her daughter's marriage and gives rise to mother-in-law jokes.

Where it is the family of a son, problems are even more likely to arise, for although the services of a grandmother as dogsbody may be equally in demand, the daughter-in-law is less likely to share the grandmother's views on the proper running of a house, the upbringing of children and the treatment of a husband. Some women with no man of their own may be rather too interested in the welfare of their sons and criticize their wives' behaviour. Such a situation may lead to the grandmother being exploited as a home help initially, but later on, if troubles arise, she may be excluded from the son's family and not allowed to have contact with her grandchildren. This is a threat that can always be used to intimidate a woman who loves her grandchildren and wishes to be concerned with their growing up.

The chief weakness of an arrangement whereby a grandmother goes to live in the home of a son or daughter is that it may work very well in the short term but not in the long term. The following is an amalgam of several reported cases. A bereaved widow in her sixties who is sad and lonely is persuaded to live in the home of her married son or daughter. At first all goes well and she is glad to take on some of the responsibilities of looking after her young grandchildren; it is like being a mother again to have the toddlers around. The parents are pleased to be relieved of some of the unwelcome household chores, but after a while it becomes apparent that Granny is trying to run the household her way and to bring up the children according to standards that are different from those of their parents. Where such situations develop, even in quite loving families, a rift may develop to the extent that Granny needs to find a new home and is forbidden to have much contact with her grandchildren.

Managing elderly single parents

One of the forms of exploitation of a single grandmother (or a grandfather) refers to the question of 'managing' a single parent. Elderly, and to some extent vulnerable, parents may be subject to a certain amount of emotional pressure and even polite bullying from their middle-aged children. Where they shall live, how they shall manage their finances, what sort of holidays they shall take may all become the subject of pressure from a couple ganging up against a third person who is bereaved or deserted and therefore emotionally dependent. The question may arise as to whether she shall live on her own or sell the family house (and thus swell the coffers of the family money) or live in the home of her children and be a sort of supernumerary housekeeper, resident baby-minder and maid-of-all-work. If she finds this way of life irksome, especially when it is distant from the place where she used to have a circle of old friends, she may eventually decide that she would be happier in a residential home. But that would involve paying out a considerable sum in fees and deplete the family fortunes. 'What, don't you love us any more, Granny, that you would rather go and live with strangers?' This way of managing a single old parent is of course prevented if Granny acquires a new man, or Grandfather remarries. An elderly couple is better able to unite against pressures from the younger generation.

Age gaps

It is natural that among the new love relationships that are formed in later life there will be a proportion of age-gap relationships: that is, relationships where one of the partners is considerably older than the other. All the final marriages of the people described in Chapter 5 were age-gap relationships, and all but one were highly successful. It is generally believed that almost all older men would like to take up with much younger wives or mistresses, but in fact when this has been investigated it has been found not to be true. In Starr and Weiner's study of eight hundred men and women over the age of sixty they were asked to describe the ideal lover of their fantasy.[8] Nearly a third of them did not mention any age in connection with their ideal but, where an age was mentioned, the great majority of them described someone not much different in age from themselves. Of the men responding, 32.2 per cent described an ideal woman lover as being over sixty. This is perhaps surprising in view of the fact that all these men had been subject to the usual social expectations that older men would prefer much younger women if they could get them. In fact, only 1.9 per cent of the men specified an ideal in the age range of twenty to twenty-nine years and one man specified a teenager.

The point is that in their later years most men and women have had the experience of life that leads to a realistic knowledge of what to expect of people. A partner who is much younger may prove to be rather a disappointment because he or she has not shared the social experiences of the older partner and hence be a less than adequate companion. This extends to the old and the young having different vocabularies and use of idiom. The younger partner may find that the older one uses words and discusses concepts that are outdated and the older may not appreciate the more 'streetwise' concepts of the younger partner.

Pitkeathley and Emerson, in their book *Age Gap Relationships*, present data they have collected from interviews with men and women who formed relationships with people considerably older or younger than themselves, and they discuss the advantages and disadvantages of such unions.[9] The disadvantages of the difference in social experience need not apply in all couples if they are willing and able to learn from someone of another generation, as in the following case they cite where a man was thirty years older than his wife:

> At the same time, because she is so much more in touch with the modern scene than I am, I can, at least, receive an inkling of what is going on with the younger generation. It all helps with my trying to be a bit more tolerant. We both learn about each other and our different outlooks on our life together. Well, that's the theory – mostly it works out in practice. Altogether it has been a most successful marriage and now, almost eleven years later, we are looking forward to the next eleven successful years.[10]

One of the weaknesses of the book is that the authors do not mention the actual ages of those they have interviewed, and this can be important when we are considering the love life of elderly people. In the case just cited all we are told is that the age gap was thirty years, but it makes a great deal of practical difference to the future success of the marriage if it is a man of sixty marrying a woman of thirty or a man of seventy-five marrying someone of forty-five. In the former case, after eleven years they might well look forward to 'the next eleven successful years', as many men of seventy-one are quite healthy and energetic nowadays. But if the man was seventy-five years old when he married it would be

unlikely that, if still alive at eighty-six, he would be a very adequate husband for his fifty-six-year-old wife, who would probably
be as robust and appreciative of a sex life as most other women of
that age. We have to consider the fact that in later life men dete-
riorate health-wise more rapidly than women and that as far as sex
is concerned they begin to lose both their capacity and desire at
an earlier age. A woman who married a man twenty-seven years
older than herself puts the position very well:

> Marrying a man twenty-seven years older, I always knew of course
> there was a possibility I'd be a youngish widow. But I simply never
> thought I might end up having to care for him when he became an
> invalid. But that's what happened. He had a stroke and I didn't
> become a youngish widow, I became a middle-aged carer, ageing by
> the day because of the stress of it. We were so happy together I felt
> running the risk of being a youngish widow was worth it. If you ask
> me if it was worth it to become an ageing carer, I'm not sure what
> my answer would be. You don't think about these things enough
> when you are swept off your feet by a successful older man.[11]

We have already examined the problems resulting from middle-
aged children reacting to their elderly parents forming new relationships, but when it comes to age-gap relationships hostility may
be shown by members of the family, both young and old, as is illustrated by the following case of an older woman who had married
a man much younger than herself:

> I have a daughter only one year older than him and a son four
> years younger. They took the view that if Angelo made me happy
> it was OK. His family was a different story. Quite awful. He'd had
> other older women and at first they looked on me as more of a sex-
> ual experience. They even lent us a house to meet in. But when
> they knew it was more serious, they told him I was past my sell-by

date and he should move on. They had all kinds of schemes to break us up and, by the time of our marriage, were openly hostile. They asked us not to marry, then forbade us, asked us to postpone: they were ill, we'd cause them heart attacks or even death. All the family rang us and there were threats of suicide. They even planned to kidnap him as a last ditch before the wedding. They have lost him for ever, as he has never spoken to them again. They have sent poison pen letters and turned his whole family against him. Perhaps it is because they wanted grandchildren, but the depth of their disgust is quite frightening. They say it is obscene, abnormal. I find it profoundly threatening.[12]

I have encountered such extreme cases of familial hatred in my clinical work and the surprising thing is that people who go to such bizarre lengths to show hostility do not appear to be at all abnormal superficially when one meets them socially. The whole area of sex and marriage brings out the most pathological reactions in some otherwise normal people.

Pitkeathley and Emerson's collection of interviews reveal some unexpectedly favourable assessments of age-gap relationships and show how different people are in their needs for a loving partner. Some women are happiest with a man who is much older than themselves. Even the fact of him already having children may make him especially valued, as in the following case:

Although I have had just as many relationships with men of about my own age, those in which the man was significantly older than me had, as it were, an added dimension. It's quite simple really: I've always liked having a father figure, so in these partnerships the normal man–woman relationship was overlaid with a child–parent one. In fact I was particularly attracted by men who already had children, because that seemed to add somehow to the father image that I liked to conjure up. It was a turn-on for me.[13]

In Chapter 5 the marriages of Charlie Chaplin are discussed, and his last wife Oona gives her reasons for preferring a husband who was much older than herself.

The risk of bereavement

It is obvious that if one partner is much younger than the other, she or he risks a sudden end to a happy love relationship by the death of the older partner. Such a case is illustrated in Part 2 in the account given by Gertrude, whose new-found happiness was ended by the fatal heart attack of her husband. Such a risk is inevitable and not only was Gertrude quite willing to accept it but such was her conviction that older people should live happily with a partner if they were fortunate enough to meet a suitable person that she was ready to remarry if the opportunity should arise.

We have already considered the case of a woman who married a man twenty-seven years older than herself. While she was fully prepared to become a young widow eventually, what happened was perhaps even sadder: she became a middle-aged carer to an invalid and 'ageing by the day because of the stress of it'. Some types of long-lasting and crippling terminal illness can indeed be very stressful for a carer and, while we can all face our own eventual mortality and that of our loved ones with fortitude because it is in the natural order of things, the cruel fate of a chronic illness that is lingering and destructive may be worse than bereavement in some cases.

In conclusion, that age-gap relationships raise special issues is undeniable, but people are so different in their practical and emotional needs that one cannot lay down invariable principles. It is best to be aware of the various problems that may arise and judge each individual case on its own merits.

CHAPTER 5

Four late marriages

In this chapter we shall look at the cases of four well-known people who remarried in later life. I have chosen four famous people because a considerable amount is known about their lives: Bertrand Russell, Charlie Chaplin, George Eliot (Mary Ann Evans) and Colette (Sidonie Gabrielle Colette). The common denominator that runs through the lives of all of them is a hunger for love that persisted right into their old age; for three of them the most successful of their loves came in later life, and for one of them it was a disaster.

Bertrand Russell (1872–1970)

Critics of Bertrand Russell have sometimes scoffed at his being regarded as an authority on marriage in view of the fact that he was divorced three times. The basis of his reputation lies in some of his writings, especially his book *Marriage and Morals.*[1] Looking at his domestic career we may regard it as much the same as many people's: a pilgrimage, a search for fulfilment in love. He began his autobiography with the following passage:

Three passions, simple but overwhelmingly strong, have governed my life: the longing for love, the search for knowledge and unbearable pity for the suffering of mankind. These passions, like great winds, have blown me hither and thither in a wayward course, over a deep ocean of anguish, reaching to the very verge of despair.

I have sought love first, because it brings ecstasy: ecstasy so

91

great that I would often have sacrificed all my life for a few hours of this joy. I have sought it next, because it relieves loneliness: that terrible loneliness in which one shivering consciousness looks over the rim of the world into the cold unfathomable lifeless abyss. I have sought it finally, because in the union of love I have seen, in a mystic miniature, the prefiguring heaven that saints and poets have imagined. This is what I sought, and though it might seem too good for human life, this is what – at last – I have found.[2]

The triumphant ending of this passage, which was written when he was aged ninety-four, refers to his final marriage to Edith Finch, which brought him domestic happiness for the last eighteen years of his life.

Russell had a very chequered love life, much of which is recorded with amazing frankness in his autobiography, but here I will simply discuss his four marriages.

Russell first met Alys Pearsall Smith when he was aged seventeen and she was twenty-two, and according to him he felt 'love at first sight'. She was a very beautiful woman, the daughter of an American couple who had settled in this country, and with their background of New England Quakers provided a welcome challenge to the young Russell, who was a member of the Whig aristocracy. According to his biographer Caroline Moorhead, 'Even by the rigid morality of the day, Alys and Russell were, by temperament as well as upbringing, extraordinarily prudish. For all the outpourings on paper, it was not until . . . almost five years after their first meeting, that they kissed.'[3]

Russell's grandmother, who had brought him up as his own mother had died when he was very young, was strongly opposed to his marrying Alys, whom she regarded as a schemer with 'distinctly common' parents. She told her grandson that Alys was, 'no lady, a baby-snatcher, a low-class adventuress, a person incapable of finer feelings, a woman whose vulgarity would perpetually put me to shame'.[4] While Lady Russell's aristocratic prejudices were not entirely justified, as Alys was merely a typical American woman of her class and time, devoted to good works and trying to better herself intellectually, it must be admitted that many of Russell's friends and acquaintances found her pretty intolerable. His colleague and collaborator Alfred Whitehead gave as his reason for disliking her, 'She's such an awful liar.'

A number of affectionate letters from Russell to his wife attest to the fact that for about five years things went quite well between them, but in his autobiography he tells of a strange incident:

> I went out bicycling one afternoon and suddenly, as I was riding along a country road, I realized that I no longer loved Alys. I had had no idea until this moment that my love for her was even lessening. The problem presented by this discovery was very grave . . . At this crisis my father's priggery came out in me, and I began to justify myself with moral criticisms of Alys. I did not at once tell her that I no longer loved her, but of course she perceived that something was amiss. She retired to a rest-cure for some months, and when she emerged from it I told her I no longer wished to share a room, and in the end I confessed that my love was dead. I justified this attitude to her, as well as to myself, by criticisms of her character.[5]

What he does not reveal in his autobiography, but what various biographers have discovered in their research, is that at this time Russell had fallen deeply in love with somebody else. He confessed this some years later to his friend and lover Ottoline Morrell, but he did not reveal just who this 'somebody' was. Subsequent researchers have revealed that she was Evelyn Whitehead, the wife of his colleague, a woman who was to have a profound influence on his moral development and occasion in him what he refers to as his 'conversion'. It occurred when he found Evelyn in a paroxysm of pain during a hysterical heart attack, and this led him to have an almost mystical experience.

> Suddenly the ground seemed to give way beneath me and I found myself in quite another region. Within five minutes I went through some such reflections as the following: the loneliness of the human soul is unendurable; nothing can penetrate it except the highest intensity of the sort of love that religious teachers have preached; whatever does not spring from this motive is harmful or at best useless; it follows that war is wrong, that a public school education is abominable, that the use of force is to be deprecated and that in human relations one should penetrate to the core of loneliness in each person and speak to that . . . At the end of five minutes I became a completely different person. For a time, a sort of mystic illumination possessed me. I felt that I knew the inmost thoughts of everybody that I met in the street, and though this was, no doubt, a delusion, I did in actual fact find myself in far closer touch than previously with all my friends and many of my acquaintances.[6]

This is a very odd confession of Russell's and it appears to cover up the simple fact that having fallen in love with his colleague's wife he hardly dared admit it to himself but firmly repressed it. It was the beginning of a miserable period in which he lived in celibacy although in the same house as Alys for about nine years and tried to keep up appearances in a marriage that had utterly failed. During these years he buried himself in intense intellectual work and produced the successive volumes of his great work of mathematical philosophy, the *Principia Mathematica*, in collaboration with Alfred Whitehead. His undeclared love for Evelyn slowly died.

I do not propose to mention all the love affairs that Russell had during his long life but simply to deal with those that gave rise to his marriages. His affair with Ottoline Morrell, however, is in a special category in that she was instrumental in emancipating him from the priggish and ultra-puritan conditioning that had dominated him up to the age of about thirty-nine. Certainly, when he got to know Ottoline he was no longer the immature and emotionally undeveloped boy that he had been when he married Alys, but as well as his quite remarkable intellect he had a huge potential for passionate expression that had not yet been released.

Ottoline was the wife of Philip Morrell, a Liberal politician, and as a couple they were very fond of each other, but she had led an unusual life among the upper-class literary and artistic intelligentsia and her husband tolerated her various affairs. Russell was a type of person quite new to her, as she was to him. At first she was rather intimidated by his tremendous intellectual reputation and powerful personal charisma. She wrote in her diary, 'I don't think I have ever met anyone more attractive, but very charming, so quick and clear-sighted and supremely intellectual. His notice flattered me very much – but still I trembled at it feeling that in half an hour he would see how silly one was and despise me.'[7] They fell in love and had a tumultuous affair that lasted about six years. Russell's curious mixture of sexual passion and intellectualizing gave rise to his writing her nearly a thousand love letters during one year, surely a record in the annals of amatory correspondence.

The affair lasted for nearly six years, but after a short stay in America Russell returned to find that Ottoline had decided to end it as far as love-making went. They continued to be good friends and kept in touch with one another until she died at the age of sixty-four. Russell described her influence on him thus:

She laughed at me when I behaved like a don or a prig. She gradually cured me of the belief that I was seething with appalling wickedness that could only be kept under by an iron self-control. She made me less self-centred, and less self-righteous . . . She made me less of a Puritan.[8]

Thus Russell in his mid-forties, when many men are settling down to a more staid way of life, became a very different man from the inhibited Cambridge don he had been in the first part of his life. He was now getting into his stride as a writer, exerting a libertarian and humanistic influence on a wide range of topics that made him a figure known throughout the world.

Russell's next marriage to Dora Black was never a marriage in the accepted sense, although it was duly registered after his divorce from Alys. In her autobiographical book *The Tamarisk Tree* Dora wrote:

> I married him at his urgent request to legitimize our son, on the understanding that this marriage was not to be regarded in the orthodox legal sense. I did not lay claim to object to his infidelities, nor to forgive him for them. I did not hold that they required forgiveness. The possessive tone of 'my wife', 'my husband' did not exist in my vocabulary.[9]

In view of Dora's statement it is perhaps surprising that the marriage lasted as long as eight years, three of them being spent in separation and a very sad wrangle over a divorce. Their association started very happily, living openly as unmarried lovers, and during the marriage both of them had outside affairs which apparently created no friction. They had two children, John and Kate, and then Dora had a child by one of her lovers, an American journalist, Griffin Barry. They appear to have ceased having sexual relations two years after the marriage. Some biographers have suggested that Russell became impotent with Dora, although he was later to father a child by his third wife. On hearing that Dora had conceived a child by Barry, Russell wrote on 14 November 1929:

My Darling Love

I got your letter this morning . . . I should not like you to do anything about it – if it is so, much better to let nature take its course. Since I cannot do my part, it is better someone else should, as you ought to have more children. But I dare say it was a false alarm. In any case there is no need to worry, you won't find me tiresome about it.

I am glad everything goes well at the school. It is so much better than last time! A month from today I sail – I shall be glad.

My love, Darling. No time for more. B.[10]

Barry's daughter, Harriet, was registered as Russell's child (hence getting into *Debrett's Peerage*) and was at first brought up with the other two children, but after a few years Dora and Russel began to quarrel, the main bone of contention being the experimental school which they had begun together at Beacon Hill. It had become more and more Dora's concern, Russell maintaining that the experiment had failed and that they should close the school; but she was determined to carry on with it and to subsidize it financially if necessary. When Dora had her second child by Barry, Russell left the school for good and set up house with a young woman who had been his mistress for some years, Peter Spence.

With hindsight, one cannot be other than glad that Dora and Russell split up when they did, for if he had gone on managing the school in partnership one of the greatest intellects of this century – and subsequent winner of the Nobel Peace Prize – would have spent his days educating a small number of schoolchildren.

Russell was aged sixty-three and Peter (Marjorie) Spence

twenty-five when he married her in 1936, a year after his second divorce. For some years the marriage was very successful, she being a competent and energetic woman, acting as his secretary and general manager in a period during which he was extremely busy with his writing and lecturing. They had one son, Conrad, who proved to be a very intelligent and precocious child.

Russell and Peter spent some years together in America, where he held a series of academic appointments at different universities, including the farcical interlude following his appointment to a professorship at New York City College. There a confederation of Catholics and moral crusaders launched a campaign against Russell, accusing him of every sort of moral turpitude and succeeded in having the appointment quashed, a furore that became a nationwide *cause célèbre*. At his next appointment at the Barnes Foundation, Philadelphia, Peter began to show signs of mental depression and strange behaviour. She had never been an easy person to get along with, and her behaviour became so eccentric that she was actually barred from entering the campus where her husband was lecturing.

In the early years of their marriage she had been a great asset to Russell, not only as a devoted wife and competent secretary but as a defender against much of the hostility with which he was faced. Biographers are rather puzzled about what was wrong with Peter, but as she grew older she became very moody and withdrawn and began to quarrel with many of Russell's academic and personal friends. In the end her hostility was turned against Russell himself and she left him, taking their son with her. For many years the son sided with his mother and would not see Russell, but when he was aged thirty he became reconciled with his father, upon which Peter disowned him. According to Caroline Moorhead, 'once she knew that Conrad, on his way to becoming a successful and respected historian, was seeing his father, she became more solitary, refusing even to see her son. No one is sure whether she is still alive.'[11]

When Russell was aged eighty he married Edith Finch, an American writer and academic who was aged fifty-three, Peter having divorced him for desertion earlier the same year. This marriage lasted eighteen years until his death in 1970 and all biographers who have mentioned this marriage are agreed that this was his most successful.

A tribute has been paid to Edith by Russell's daughter Katharine who, rather surprisingly, was a Christian missionary. In her book *My Father: Bertrand Russell* she wrote:

> Without her I do not know how he would have survived the personal and global anxieties that beset the last twenty years of his life . . . I do not know Edith very well for I was not often in England during these years, and she is as shy as I am, but all that I know I like. If I could have ordered for him from the Almighty a person to accompany my father to the end of his life, it would have been someone like Edith, devoted, courageous and witty.[12]

Russell was extremely fortunate finally to have married someone like Edith, who was a strong-minded person in her own right but who shared his views on most subjects and took an active part in his campaigns. Whether their life together would have been as harmonious if they had married at an earlier period of his life is debatable. Hostile critics have made much of his womanizing, but it must be remembered that, although he was certainly not good-looking by most standards of male beauty, he had an extraordinary charisma which made many women fall for him and he was never without a circle of female admirers and potential mistresses. He was probably faithful to Edith, and she to him, after their marriage.

Edith left no autobiography, but in some notes for a speech she was to deliver after Russell's death she summed up her appreciation of him and this accords very well with what other friends of his have said. She refers to his compassion, generosity and loving nature and to his huge capacity for enjoyment of life. Russell made many enemies and they still pursue his memory beyond the grave. One thing that I have noticed is that those who preserve an implacable hostility towards him seldom mention the existence of Edith, his last wife, and the eighteen years of his one successful marriage at the end of his life.

Charlie Chaplin (1889–1977)

Charlie Chaplin came from a very humble home in south London and at one time in early boyhood lived in a workhouse. He left school at the age of twelve to earn some money and thereafter was practically self-educated. As an internationally famous entertainer he was far more widely known than Bertrand Russell. Laurence Olivier called him 'the greatest actor of all time', and his importance in the creation and development of the cinema should not be underestimated.

Both Chaplin and Russell were married four times and their last marriage in later life was far the most successful. Both men had a considerable sexual appetite and it is not known how many affairs they had in the period before their final marriage. As Chaplin lived in the film world, where sexual promiscuity was much more the norm, his first two marriages were simply the result of his lovers becoming pregnant – or appearing to be so.

Mildred Harris had been a child actress since 1910 and Chaplin married her in 1918 when she was aged seventeen and he twenty-nine. His interest in young girls was one of his characteristics: all of his four wives were teenagers when he first became involved with them. The reason for this marriage was that Mildred told him that she was pregnant and only after the marriage did this prove to be false. She was very pretty and little more need be said about her. Chaplin confided in a friend that she was 'no mental heavyweight'. The marriage lasted two years before she divorced him.

Lita Grey (Lillita McMurray) really was pregnant when Chaplin married her in 1924 when she was just seventeen, although she pretended to be nineteen for the sake of the news-paper reports; and she bore him two sons. She was the leading lady in the film *The Gold Rush* and, according to Chaplin's biog-rapher David Robinson, it was 'a marriage that was to bring more bitterness into Chaplin's life even than his time with Mildred'.[13] Such was Chaplin's unhappiness associated with this marriage that when he came to write his autobiography he said almost nothing about it. All he wrote was: 'During the filming of *The Gold Rush* I married for the second time. Because we have two grown sons of whom I am very fond, I will not go into any details. For two years we were married and tried to make a go of it, but it was hopeless and ended in a great deal of bitterness.'[14]

When petitioning for divorce Lita was to write (or had written for her) an extraordinary diatribe, fifty-two pages long, which sought to smear him and ruin his career. In it she cited 'five prominent women' with whom Chaplin was alleged to be 'inti-mate'. The judge in the case refused to hear all her unseemly alle-gations and she withdrew them, agreeing to a large cash settle-ment and the endowment of a trust fund for each child.

At the age of fourteen Paulette Goddard had been in the chorus of the Ziegfeld Follies and had married a rich playboy at the age of sixteen but divorced him before the year was ended. She was aged twenty-two when Chaplin married her in 1936, but he had been living with her for about four years before that. The marriage took place at Canton when they were away together on holiday in the Far East. This third marriage was more successful than the other two and lasted six years before she divorced him, but its success appeared to depend on their not seeing very much of each other. She had been his leading lady while filming *Modern Times*, a film which was finished before the marriage. In his autobiography Chaplin was to write:

> Paulette and I had now been married for a year, but a breach was widening between us. It was partly due to my being worried and absorbed in trying to work. However, on the success of *Modern Times* Paulette was signed up to make several pictures for Paramount, but I could neither work nor play.[15]

Paulette was quite a success with Paramount, and she and Chaplin remained friends after the divorce. He agreed to include her in his film *The Great Dictator*, although in his autobiography he says that they both knew that they would eventually separate even before this film was begun. He had no children by this marriage.

Before Chaplin's marriage to Oona O'Neill he had a narrow escape from what would have been yet another disastrous episode with an unsuitable wife. In the period after the divorce from Paulette, he was approached by a young actress called Joan Barry, who obviously hoped to marry him. At first he thought that she had considerable talent that could be developed and saw quite a lot of her as she was very attractive and undoubtedly had great potential. For a time he arranged for her to attend Max Reinhardt's drama school, paid for elaborate dental work for her and showed off her acting talents in Shakespearian parts at parties. He told his sons, 'She has a quality, an ethereal something that's truly marvellous . . . a talent as great as any I've seen in my whole life.'

Eventually it became apparent that Joan Barry was mentally unstable. She used to drive up to Chaplin's house when very drunk in the small hours of the morning and on one occasion she smashed his windows when he refused to let her in. She eventually gave birth to a baby and alleged that he was the father. Although a blood test proved that Chaplin could not have fathered the infant, in an extraordinary trial the jury disregarded such hard evidence and found in favour of Barry's claim, and an order was made for him to support the child. But at least Chaplin had grown wiser over the years and resisted getting married to her.

Chaplin's resistance to Barry's overtures coincided with his meeting Oona O'Neill. She was the daughter of Eugene O'Neill, the playwright, and at the age of sixteen arrived at Hollywood, where her mother and stepfather lived, to take a screen test for the film that was to be produced by Eugene Frenke. Her agent knew that Chaplin was looking for someone to play the role of Brigid in his projected film *Shadow and Substance* and suggested that Oona might fill it, but he was doubtful if anyone so young could take the part. After Chaplin's elder son had seen the girl he wrote:

> Whenever Oona was with our father a rapt expression would come into her eyes. She would sit quietly hanging on his every word. Most women are charmed by Dad, but in Oona's case it was different. She worshipped him, drinking in every word he spoke, whether it was about his latest script, the weather or some bit of philosophy. She seldom spoke, but every now and then she would come up with one of those penetrating remarks that impressed even our father with her insight.[16]

Chaplin married her when she was eighteen and one might have supposed that by marrying yet another teenage film actress this would be the beginning of a further disastrous marriage. In fact it proved to be a very happy marriage which lasted until he died at the age of eighty-eight. She bore him eight children, three of them conceived after he was seventy years of age.

At the age of seventy Chaplin was interviewed and recorded the following about his marriage:

I love my wife and she loves me. That is why we are so happy. If you don't demand too much from each other – that, I think, comes nearest to being a formula for happiness in marriage. The rest takes care of itself through tolerance. In the sixteen years of our marriage, we have been separated only once – for five days when Oona went on a business trip to America.

She is my inspiration and she is a good critic. She has a natural talent and her criticism is constructive. To get her reactions to anything I do I let her see my day's output of work. She never discusses anything or offers an opinion unless I ask her. Sometimes I disagree with her opinion only to find a week later that she was right.

We have a profound respect for each other's tastes and views, and this makes for a most agreeable atmosphere in the home . . . We can be thoroughly relaxed with each other and enjoy our own company without having to indulge in conversation . . . Oona feels that she has no talents except as a wife and mother.[17]

The fact is that Oona, beautiful and talented as she was, gave up all her ambitions to be a film star and settled for being a wife to Chaplin and raising a large family. They spent the latter part of his life away from the US film world, mainly living in Europe, with a base in Switzerland where Oona brought up the family.

At the time of the interview recorded above, Oona was also interviewed:

I am married to a young man. People think of Charlie as my father, but age counts for nothing in this house. To me he seems younger every day. There is certainly no father fixation about my feeling for Charlie. He has made me mature and I keep him young.

I never consciously think about Charlie's age for 364 days of the year. Only his birthday is an annual shock for me. But I can feel the way some people stare at me with puzzlement and then look back at him wondering how we have kept it up; whether it's just a façade.

My security and stability with Charlie stem not from his wealth but from the very difference in years between us. Only young women who have married mature men will know what I mean.[18]

George Eliot (1819–80)

George Eliot was a woman who, at the age of sixty, after a relatively short period of intense mourning for the man with whom she had lived happily outside wedlock for twenty-four years, suddenly got married, to the surprise of everyone who knew her. Her new husband was a man twenty years her junior and with very little to recommend him. The enigma of why she took this step has never been resolved satisfactorily, nor why the husband made a serious attempt at suicide on their honeymoon. I will attempt to offer some solutions to the puzzle and illustrate the fact that in later life some women, notwithstanding intellectual superiority, a wide circle of supportive friends and commitment to work, have a continuing need for erotic love.

George Eliot was the pen-name of Mary Ann Evans, who was later known as Marian, the name by which she will be referred to here. When her lover, George Lewes, died in November 1878 they had been living together happily as man and wife for twenty-four years. They had seemed a very well-matched couple and no one was surprised at the depth of her sorrow on bereavement. She was then at the peak of her fame, having published all her major works, and was surrounded by many good friends, both male and female. It might have been expected that in bereavement she would have devoted her time to her work and relied on the supportive society of her friends. In fact, less than a year after Lewes's death she was writing love letters to John Cross and she married him in May 1880.

Cross was not an impressive man. He was a financial broker and had been the friend and business adviser of Marian and her common-law husband for many years. They referred to him jokingly as their 'nephew' and references to him in Marian's journal are casual and formal: 'Mr Cross came to dinner', 'Eleanor Cross and her brother came to call.' There is no hint that he was anything other than a friend, much younger than her and her husband. On his side he may well have been devoted to her for a long time, and he was still a bachelor at the age of forty. He had the asset of being tall and handsome.

After their sudden marriage they went on honeymoon to Venice and there Cross attempted suicide by jumping from a balcony into the Grand Canal. He was saved from death and Kathleen Adams relates that 'he was fished out by two passing gondoliers and returned to the hotel, none the worse for his soaking but reputedly furious with his rescuers for their timely (or untimely?) intervention'.[19]

Why he tried to end his life in this way when he had only just got married to Marian, the admired friend of so many years who had shown him warm love and admitted him to her bed, will never be known. Strangely, Marian made no mention at all of the incident in her diary. The attempted suicide being hushed up completely, with Cross's brother bribing all possible witnesses to silence, Marian continued to tell her friends in her letters how well their honeymoon travels were proceeding.

Some possible lines of inquiry have tantalized biographers. Was he mentally unsound and given to suicidal behaviour? He always seemed to others to be a cheerful, busy sort of person, and he lived to the age of eighty-four without any repetition of such behaviour. In the biography of Marian that he wrote after her death, his account of this incident is totally unbelievable. In writing it he had recourse to Marian's intimate early journal, and he destroyed forty-six pages covering the years 1849–54. It is possible that this journal revealed incidents in her life that he regarded as utterly incompatible with an image of her that he wanted to convey, and if on their honeymoon she told him of things about herself that he simply could not stomach this may have accounted for his sudden despair. More simply, it may have been that he found he could not live up to her, sexually and emotionally, and a terrible sense of his own inadequacy drove him to attempt suicide. He may have thought that he had married a Victorian lady gently declining into prim old age, despite her past unconventional union, only to find that she was nothing of the sort; instead, someone who had had twenty-four years of passionate sexual experience with a well-matched partner and demanded of him something he could not give.

In order to try to get some real insight into the emotional nature of this remarkable woman, it is necessary to recount very briefly the history of her more important involvements with men, such as are known to us.

The man who appears first to have aroused Marian's amatory interest was Dr Robert Brabant, who had a medical practice in Devizes. He knew a number of interesting and influential people, including the poet Coleridge, and he appears to have been rather a poseur, affecting to have more scholarly knowledge than he had. Caroline Bray, a close friend of Marian's who exerted considerable influence over her in her younger adult life, considered Dr Bray to be a silly, vain little man.

Marian had been a bridesmaid at the wedding of Dr Brabant's daughter Rufa, and when she left for her honeymoon, Marian was invited to stay at the doctor's house to fill the gap left by Rufa's departure. This was in 1843 when Marian was aged twenty-four. She was a very plain young woman, awkward in her social manners but already showing signs of a brilliant and formidable capacity for intellectual work. That she was impressed by the pretentious doctor was partly due to her social inexperience, his façade of learning and his name-dropping of famous people whose acquaintance he cultivated. Undoubtedly there was also a strong sexual attraction between them that was all too apparent to others. He was then aged sixty-one and married to a woman who had lost her sight some years before and whom he treated as a nonentity.

Marian wrote to her friend Caroline Bray:

> I am in a little heaven here, Dr Brabant being its archangel . . . time would fail me to tell of all his charming qualities. We read and walk and talk together, and I am never weary of his company. I have just written to Father to beg for a longer leave of absence than I thought of when I came. I am petted and fed with nice morsels and pretty speeches until I am in danger of becoming more conceited than ever.[20]

She was encouraged to consider the library as her own, a room to which other female members of the household were not welcome. Her intimate association with Dr Brabant involved their reading Greek together and her reading German to him. They also went on long walks and at times she said that she felt so faint that she had to lie down on a sofa to rest, with the doctor in attendance at her side. The situation that developed in the household was rather similar to that depicted by Ibsen in *The Master Builder*, when the young woman Hilde comes to stay in the house of the ageing Halvard Solnes and arouses the jealousy of his wife. In this instance, however, Marian was infinitely superior intellectually to the ageing husband. Although Mrs Brabant was blind, she sensed what was going on and her formidable sister Mrs Hughes was in the house and reporting to her how the situation was developing. Marian had intended to stay for six weeks, but before two weeks had passed Mrs Hughes was officiously advising her on the best way by which she could return to Coventry, and the situation became so tense that she was forced to leave.

Over a year later, Rufa Hennell, the daughter of the house, wrote to a friend, John Chapman, exonerating Marian on the grounds of the 'simplicity of her heart and ignorance of the required conventions'. Rufa wrote:

> Miss Evans left. Mrs B. vowed that she should never enter the house again, or that if she did, she, Mrs Brabant, would instantly leave it. Mrs Hennell says Dr B. acted ungenerously and worse towards Miss E., for though he was the chief cause of all that passed, he acted towards her as though the fault lay with her alone. His unmanliness in the affair was condemned more by Mrs Hennell than by Miss E. herself. [21]

It is of interest that John Chapman, the recipient of Rufa's confidences, was later to recreate the same situation in his own household in the Strand where Marian came as a lodger in 1851 and aroused the jealousy of his wife and his live-in mistress! Marian put her experiences at Devizes to good use years later when she used aspects of Dr Brabant's character as a basis for Mr Casaubon in her novel *Middlemarch*.

In 1845 when Marian was aged twenty-six and staying with her half-sister Mrs Houghton, she met a young man, a painter and picture restorer, whose name is unknown. After spending two days in his company she said that 'she thought him the most interesting young man that she had seen, and superior to all the rest of mankind'. Her biographer Gordon Haight writes:

> The young man was so smitten with her that he got his host, Henry Houghton, to convey a proposal that he might be allowed to pay court to her, with the eventual object of marriage, saying, 'she was the most fascinating creature he had ever beheld, that if it were not

too presumptuous to hope . . . etc., etc. . . .' He must have been a very impressionable young man to consider proposing so soon, in view of Marian's plainness but, despite her very big nose and prominent lower jaw, she did exert a strange fascination over men. Marian gave him permission to write to her and went to see Caroline Bray and her husband 'brimful of happiness'. She said that she had not fallen in love with him yet, but admired his character so much that she was sure that she would.[22]

One can well imagine that any personable young man who approached her at this time with offers of love so suddenly and intensely would have had a considerable impact on the love-hungry Marian. She showed his letters to the Brays and they were quite favourably impressed by them. Eventually the young artist called to see Marian at the Brays' house, but he was so agitated and diffident that he created a poor impression and she was disappointed in him. The image that she had created of him being very interesting was patently false, the product of her own intense need. She confided in her friends that she now thought that she could never come to love and respect him enough to marry him and wrote to break off the association.

John Chapman was the recipient of Rufa Hennell's (née Brabant) confidences about Marian's abortive affair with her father, and there is no doubt that Chapman greatly looked forward to meeting the interesting Miss Evans. He was a good-looking young man with an unusual background. Originally apprenticed as a watchmaker, he had been a dealer in timepieces and similar instruments and at one time had studied medicine. He had used his good looks to captivate a rich manufacturer's daughter, fourteen years older than himself, thereby acquiring a useful amount of capital. He then turned his hand to writing and produced rather a strange philosophical book, the product of his attempted self-education. When he sent it to a London publisher, the latter suggested that he produce the book himself and offered to sell him his publishing business. Chapman bought the firm with his wife's money and in the capacity of a new publisher he cultivated the society of writers, attracting them with lavish parties at his house, which became a centre of the literary scene. He further expanded his enterprise by setting up a high-class boarding house, eventually moving to premises in the Strand where the lower part was devoted to the publishing business and the upper floors the living quarters.

Marian's first contact with him was through her having translated Friedrich Strauss's great work *Das Leben Jesu*, a labour that occupied her for two years. For all this work Chapman paid her £20. He was apt to exploit his women friends both sexually and financially.

Chapman lived with his wife Susanna, their two children and Elizabeth Tilley, a pretty young woman who lived in the house as a domestic helper, governess to the children and mistress to John Chapman. That she was his regular mistress is beyond doubt, for when his diary was examined in this century it was found that he recorded the occurrence of her menstrual periods.

Apparently his wife tolerated the presence of one mistress living in the house, but when he took Marian into the house as a lodger in February 1851 the situation became intolerable. It is unlikely that he ever succeeded in making Marian his mistress, but she became very emotionally involved with him and this caused jealous scenes between the three women. After just over a month she had to leave to relieve the tension, Elizabeth Tilley being even more jealous than his wife. Chapman recorded rather smugly in his diary:

Monday, 24th March, 1851. M. departed today, I accompanied her to the railway. She was very sad and hence made me feel so. She pressed me for some intimation of the state of my feelings, I told her that I felt great affection for her, but that I loved E. and S. also, though each in a different way. At this avowal she burst into tears.

I tried to comfort her and reminded [her] of the dear friends and pleasant home she was returning to, but the train whirled her away very, very sad.[23]

Such was Chapman's power over the three women that when he had an economic motive for reinstating Marian in the household he managed it successfully. It is possible that, confirmed philanderer and seducer as he was with plenty of women available to him, he had little sexual interest in Marian but used his considerable charm to exploit her great literary ability. He bought the *Westminster Review* as a business venture shortly after Marian had left for Coventry and then had some difficulty in finding an editor. Marian seemed a suitable choice if only he could persuade her to take on the job and come back to live in London. His charm worked again; not only did he get her to agree to return to his house in the Strand but he talked his wife and Elizabeth into accepting her return on his solemn promise that there would be no more philandering with her and that their relations would be strictly businesslike. It says something for Marian's need to be wanted, even without any erotic reward, that she was able to swallow her pride and return to the house that she had been forced to leave. We may wonder at Mrs Chapman's complaisance in the matter, but it has been suggested that if Marian had lived anywhere else in London she knew that her husband might get up to his old tricks, perhaps under the guise of editorial meetings, but if she had the younger woman living under the same roof she could keep a close eye on what was going on.

It may be thought that Marian would have been desperately miserable living in the house of the man she loved but could not have and seeing him interact with his two other women, but fortunately she was soon to fall in love with a friend of Chapman's, Herbert Spencer.

Herbert Spencer has been described as a 'cold fish'. Unlike

Chapman, he was a man of considerable intellect and hence able to appreciate Marian and to talk with her as an equal. He formed an affectionate friendship with her but had no wish at all to reciprocate her passion for him or become involved with her erotically. In terms of John Lee's analysis of types of love discussed in Chapter 1, his feelings for her were pure *Storge*. In theory he claimed that he approved of marriage and in later life he said that it was Marian's unprepossessing looks that prevented him from forming any closer relationship with her. In reality he appears to have had very little sex drive and he died a bachelor.

Marian's love for Spencer was that of a normal woman and she desperately hoped that eventually he would return it. She gave some evidence in her bitter letters to friends that she feared that her unprepossessing face was what deterred him. When she realized that he would never be interested in her as a lover, she determined to suppress her passionate feelings and take what consolation she could from their intellectual companionship. Yet with all her self-discipline, her hunger to be loved broke through her habitual restraint and she wrote him a pathetic letter in July 1852:

> I know this letter will make you very angry with me, but wait a little, and don't say anything to me while you are angry. I promise not to sin any more in the same way . . . I want to know if you can assure me that you will not forsake me, that you will always be with me as much as you can and share your thoughts and feelings with me. If you become attached to someone else, then I must die, but until then I could gather courage to work and make life valuable, if only I had you near me. I do not ask you to sacrifice anything – I would be very good and cheerful and never annoy you. But I find it impossible to contemplate life under any other conditions. If I had your assurance, I could trust that and live upon it. I have struggled – indeed I have – to renounce everything and be entirely

unselfish, but I find myself utterly unequal to it. Those who have known me best have always said, that if ever I loved anyone thoroughly my whole life must turn upon that feeling, and I find they said truly. You curse the destiny which has made the feeling concentrate on you but if you will only have patience with me you shall not curse it long. You will find that I can be satisfied with very little, if I am delivered from the dread of losing it.

I suppose no woman before ever wrote such a letter as this – but I am not ashamed of it, for I am conscious that in the light of reason and true refinement I am worthy of your respect and tenderness, whatever gross men or vulgar-minded women might think of me.[24]

There is no record of the letter that Herbert Spencer may have sent in reply, but fortunately it was not long before another man came into her life, someone who was to fulfil completely her great need to receive and give love in all its aspects. Their loving relationship lasted until his death twenty-four years later. This was George Lewes, with whom she began living in 1854.

Conventional good looks are not always the basis of attractiveness. Marian was held by some to be positively ugly, yet she had a strange physical attractiveness for some people. In his biography of her, Haight lists ten women who were susceptible to 'George Eliot's extraordinary attraction for women', and some of them wished to form 'a passionate friendship' with her.[25] One of them, Edith Simcox, tried to shower her with ardent kisses and had been known to greet her by kissing her feet. Yet Marian appears to have had no lesbian inclinations at all. In her, George Lewes met his true match. He too was deemed by many people to be ugly, but all were agreed that he was extremely lively and entertaining and he had an aura of animal attractiveness about him. Lewes had had a most unconventional marriage in which he shared his wife's favours with a friend and she had borne two children by this friend. Because he had condoned his wife's adultery, it was impossible for them to get a divorce, hence he and Marian had to live in sin, as it was then considered, for the whole of their association. We are told by Eliza Lynn Linton, a contemporary novelist:

> Frankly sensual, frankly self-indulgent and enjoying life, he was the born Epicurean – the natural Hedonist. Life to him meant love and pleasure, and he had that bright, expansive quality which makes pleasure and finds it everywhere, in work and in idleness, in the sans façon of Bohemianism and in the more orderly amusements of conventional society – in scientific discussion and in empty persiflage, he was equally at home, and wherever he went there was a patch of sunshine in the room. [26]

Apparently this randy, lively little man, who had a loving heart and considerable intellectual ability, was just what Marian needed to release the immense creativity that was latent within her. In the years following her going to live with Lewes she began to write the novels for which she is famous. He appears to have been utterly devoted to her and completely faithful for the rest of his life. Many commentators have remarked that we owe the novels of George Eliot to the man who gave her such abundant love during the most creative period of her career.

Some commentators have referred to the seven-month period of marriage to John Cross before she died as being 'happy'. An alternative view is that the marriage was a terrible mistake and that, although one cannot assign her death directly to any one cause, her disastrous marriage caused her health to go into a decline, culminating in her death in December apparently from a sore throat and some continuing kidney trouble. Her health had always been rather uncertain and she was afflicted with severe headaches and many psychosomatic symptoms, which varied in accordance with her emotional life. All commentators are agreed that she was always very hungry for love, but it may be remarked that in her bereaved state she was surrounded by many good friends and a number of affectionate women who would have been only too glad to be allowed to show more love for her. It is quite clear, however, that the sort of love that Marian needed was that which only a man in his capacity of husband or lover could give her. She needed erotic heterosexual love such as that she had received from George Lewes. Why then was John Cross such a failure, if indeed it was a despairing realization of his own inadequacy that made him attempt suicide on the honeymoon?

In many ways Cross was the antithesis of Lewes. In writing a biography of Marian and publishing a selection of her letters, he shows the sort of man he was: an extraordinary Victorian prude.[27] He admitted that he altered the letters he published, so that in places we do not read what Marian actually wrote but what he thought would be a more ladylike expression of feeling and opinion. Haight has made a study of these alterations and deletions and reveals Cross's absurdly prudish attitude, in one place substituting 'fingers' for 'toes', because he considered it indelicate for Victorian ladies to refer to their feet! Cross's biography is extremely dishonest and he omits entirely any account of her early relations with John Chapman. The destruction of forty-six pages of her early journal is, of course, a terrible act of literary vandalism, but Cross would have considered such an act justified if the contents offended his sense of decency.

The unhappy end of Marian's life highlights a number of important lessons that we have learned in more recent times. Some women, even when they are quite elderly, need to give and receive love just as much as when they were young. Love is not a simple concept; the kind of love that Marian needed was full-blooded erotic love, such as was appropriate for her passionate nature. Although John Cross may have loved her quite deeply, it may not have been the kind of love that she needed, and indeed it is ludicrous to suppose that a prudish man such as he could in any way have taken the place of George Lewes without causing her the most bitter disappointment.

It would appear that forming a new and successful love relationship in later life is dependent on the type of love which is given and sought.

Colette (1873–1954)

There are some superficial similarities between the late loves of George Eliot and Colette and some great contrasts. By the time they reached their sixties both women were famous writers with previous experience of erotic love, and their marriages were to men very much younger than themselves. John Cross, whom the former married at the age of sixty, was a man of no distinction who had been her financial adviser and an admirer for many years but who had no previous erotic involvement with her; Maurice Goudeket, whom Colette married at the age of sixty-one, was an established writer and had been her lover for some years before. Both men wrote posthumous biographies of their wives, but whereas Cross's biography is now dismissed as a travesty of the truth Goudeket's *Près de Colette* is accepted as an excellent portrait of her.[28] But the chief contrast is, of course, that the late-life marriage of George Eliot was a disaster and only lasted seven months until her death, whereas Colette's final marriage was long lasting and brought her a great deal of happiness and fulfilment in comparison with her two previous marriages.

The contrasts between these marriages may partly be attributed to the different periods at which the two women lived. Although George Eliot was a woman before her time who was prepared to flout convention in living outside wedlock with George Lewes for twenty-four years, the man she married was a typically conventional and prudish Victorian male who was incapable of living up to her expectations. Colette, however, lived most of her life in the twentieth century and participated in the great change in social and sexual mores that has taken place in this period, although she was always, like George Eliot, a woman before her time who shocked the conventional world by her writings and her lifestyle.

Colette became the most famous French writer of this century and was accorded many honours by her country, including being made a Grand Officer of the Legion of Honour and receiving a state funeral at her death. Much of her work was autobiographical and, unlike many of the other French writers of her time, she embraced no particular ideology – political or religious – in her work. Instead, she was committed to celebrating the joys and sadness of human life and especially the experience of love in all its forms, including love for animals and for the countryside. It was natural, therefore, that she needed both to give and to receive abundant love in her old age, and even when she was grey, wrinkled and disabled with arthritis she exuded attractiveness. In her career as a dancer and actress she gained the reputation of being both ostentatiously lesbian and sexually promiscuous with men, but apparently this was not the case. She was never unfaithful to a man with whom she was sleeping and she was quite moral and consistent according to her own personal standards.

Colette was married at the age of twenty, when she was a very unsophisticated country girl, to Henry Gauthier-Villars (Willy), a Parisian journalist and free-booting bohemian and womanizer who treated her extremely badly. He is notorious for having published her early writings, the *Claudine* books and some subsequent works, under his own name and pocketing the royalties. Such was his emotional and physical neglect of her that she became seriously ill over a long period and was only restored to health by the intervention of her devoted mother, who came to Paris to nurse her. Colette was undoubtedly deeply in love and utterly dominated by Willy for many years and seriously traumatized by his treatment of her.

The marriage with Willy lasted for thirteen years and made a deep impression on Colette throughout her subsequent life. This experience of him taught her that women should know that there is a certain sort of man whose nature they should understand. In her book *Le Pur et l'impur* she wrote:

> That man always comes into our lives more than once. His second apparition is less frightening, for we had thought him unique in the art of pleasing and destroying; by reappearing he loses stature . . . he knows that he is stripped of his powers the moment a woman, in talking about him, says 'they' instead of 'he'.[29]

On the positive side, her experience of Willy started her career as a writer and he discovered and developed her talent. It was his custom to employ various impecunious writers to produce work for him, which he would then pass off as his own, knowing, with his journalistic connections, where to get them accepted for publication. He thought he might as well employ his wife as a writing hack, getting her to write about her girlhood. Thus the *Claudine* books came into being. Once he realized how successful her writing was, he made her work several hours a day on material that he published under his own name. It was not until twelve years after her marriage to Willy that Colette published anything with her name on it and two years after that she and Willy separated. She divorced him when she was aged thirty-six after sixteen years of an unhappy marriage, during which she had been faithful to him.

It seemed likely that Colette would react from her unhappy experience of Willy by turning to lesbianism. For a while she sought solace with a group of women who affected a sapphic style of life to the extent that Lepine, the Paris Prefect of Police, had to forbid them wearing men's clothes in public to avoid scandal, such was the state of public opinion in Paris at the time. Her particular lover was the Marquise de Belbeuf, who was reputed to have left her husband after a traumatic night with him and eschewed the company of men thereafter. The Marquise wore a masculine style of dress and was generally known as 'Missy'; she was very protective towards Colette and had her to stay at her house, sleeping in the same bed. For a while the latter wore a bracelet on which was engraved 'I belong to Missy'. Soon after Colette had begun her stage career, she appeared in a mime ballet at the Moulin-Rouge called *Rêve d'Egypte* with Missy, who played the part of her male lover. When Colette embraced her with a voluptuous kiss on the stage the audience was outraged and made a noisy demonstration that brought the show to an end, Missy's husband the Marquis and his friends being in attendance in the stalls. The Prefect of Police forbade the continuance of the performance of *Rêve d'Egypte* until its name was changed, and a male actor took Missy's role.

Willy afterwards claimed that it was 'the Scandal of the Moulin-Rouge', as it was called, which made him insist on a separation from his 'vicious' wife. Actually it was he who had insisted that Colette should spice up her writing by introducing the lesbian theme into her early *Claudine* books, causing both scandal and increased sales. Biographers have cast doubt as to whether there was anything physically sexual in the love between Colette and Missy and attributed it more to Colette's need for maternal affection after her emotionally bruising years with Willy. Colette's mother, who remained her confidante and adviser for many years, indeed approved of Missy's relationship with her daughter.

According to Colette:

I was not fooled for long by these photographs that show me wearing a stiff, mannish collar, necktie and short jacket over a straight shirt, a lighted cigarette between two fingers . . . How timid I was

at that period when I was trying to look like a boy, and how femi-
nine I was beneath my disguise of cropped hair.[30]

Missy recognized that her friend was basically heterosexual and
when Colette became platonically involved with August Heriot, a
close companion in her theatrical touring company, she prepared
a 'conjugal room' for them to share when they were to visit her,
entirely mistaking the nature of their relationship. Colette wrote
to her friend Léon Hamel, 'That in itself is enough to put me off
him.'[31]

Colette possessed a powerful love of life and had a passionately
erotic nature. Thus she was not permanently put off heterosexual
love by her experiences with Willy. Two years after the divorce she
married Henry de Jouvenal, the co-editor of *Le Matin*, a paper to
which she contributed as a journalist. He was a man with aristocratic connections whom she described as 'tender, jealous, unso-
ciable and incurably honest'. The match was perhaps surprising
from his point of view as he obviously regarded it as marrying
beneath his social status, an aspect of him that Colette regarded as
absurd. During a quarrel with him she wrote to a friend: 'Alas, I
miss him terribly. His presence . . . his warmth, the sound of his
voice, his vanity, his childishness and his ridiculousness.' It was
these human qualities that endeared the man to her, and we may
compare her attachment to him with Monica's account of her
lover in Part 2 of this book as being just 'awful'.

This second marriage of Colette's lasted just eleven years, during which she gave birth to her only child, a daughter, of whom she
was very fond but neglected because of her many other commitments, leaving the child largely in the care of an English nanny.
Henry had an active love life elsewhere, and it was after they had
ceased to have sexual relations that Colette seduced Henry's older
son Bertrand by a previous marriage. In his memoirs Bertrand de
Juvenal suggested that it was this affair that led to the divorce

between his father and Colette,[32] but his half-brother, Renaud, suggested that it was Henry's mother who broke up the marriage because she wished him to marry the Princess Bibesco. He wrote:

> Did she play a part in the divorce? I don't know, but it is possible because she had an overwhelming love for her son Henry . . . and liked to interfere in other people's affairs. And it is unlikely that she would have appreciated Colette's rather uncouth manners. Her letters prove that she was delighted to welcome my father home when he left . . . she had her own candidate, the Princess Marthe Bibesco . . . and if she'd been given the slightest occasion to disturb the Henry–Colette set-up she would certainly not have let it pass.[33]

Maurice Goudeket was a naturalized Frenchman of Dutch–Jewish parents who had hoped to become a writer but who earned a living by selling pearls and other jewellery, an occupation that gave him an entrée into wealthy houses. He was aged thirty-five when he first met Colette, a bachelor and very handsome and well liked by women. On first meeting he did not much take to her and perceived her as playing a part to fit the considerable reputation that she had achieved as a writer and stage celebrity. It was two years after her divorce from Henry de Jouvenel and she was fifty-two years of age. It is not clear just when Maurice first became her lover, but they did not settle down together for some time and endured several separations. They married in 1935 when Colette was aged sixty-one, and for the next nineteen years they were a most devoted couple until her death. Colette never wavered in her love and loyalty to her husband. During the German occupation of Paris, Maurice, being Jewish, was interned for a while. He managed to secure his release before the real pogrom began and escaped to the zone in the South which was at that time unoccupied. Later during the war, however, he made his way back to Paris to resume living in secret with Colette with the help and connivance of many friends and neighbours.

One of Colette's biographers, Herbert Lottman, describes their relationship thus:

> Abundant correspondence survives attesting to Colette's adoration of her Maurice. He himself published extracts of her tender letters from Saint-Tropez. 'Hearing your voice makes me angry,' she declares in one of them. 'Within reach and out of reach at the same time. Oh, how I detest the telephone. Don't forget to telephone me on Wednesday. I'm being unreasonable, but it's hard to live without you in so lovely a place.' He never stopped being a model lover, quiet and suave.[34]

In her later life Colette became disabled with arthritis and lived for a number of years in constant pain, but Maurice never left her side, utterly devoted to her and doing his best to see that she lived as full a life as possible. In the annals of great love stories there are few to match the great attachment between Colette and Maurice in the last decades of her life. He became a successful writer and publisher, and his book *Près de Colette* is acknowledged to be an accurate account of their time together.

The loves that developed late in some of the lives of the people described in this chapter would seem to support Bashevis Singer's assertion that the art of love matures with age and experience. Of course, not everyone is fortunate in finding a suitable partner later on in life, as in the case of George Eliot. Here was a woman so passionate and so in need of a man's love after the death of her long-term lover George Lewes that she seized on the first available man, although he proved to be quite unsuitable a match for her. In Part 2 we shall read some frank first-hand accounts of men and women who have sought love in later life in a variety of circumstances.

CHAPTER 6

Staying together

Up till now the topic of love in later life has been discussed as though it were solely a matter of people forming new love relationships – indeed, all the autobiographical accounts in Part 2 concern relationships of this type. However, the norm is for the relationships in later life to be a continuation of marriages that have been in existence for many years. It is therefore worth considering how satisfactory these well-established partnerships are and what factors make for the preservation – or even the revival – of the various forms of love within them.

The traditional view is that love fades with age and that partners stay together from habit and for social and economic convenience.

Robert Browning's *Rabbi ben Ezra* offers the religious view of old love: that as marriages are divinely ordained, the last years of them are as sacrosanct and important as the earlier ones:

> Grow old along with me!
> The best is yet to be,
> The last of life, for which the first was made:
> Our times are in His hand
> Who saith, 'A whole I planned,
> Youth shows but half; trust God: see all nor be afraid!'[1]

As we have seen, most aspects of old age have been viewed very mournfully in the past, from the *Book of Ecclesiastes* onwards, because until comparatively recent times the later years of life were associated with infirmity, economic and social deprivation. Love, particularly in its ludic and erotic aspects, was regarded as a luxury to be enjoyed only by the young, and the constant theme of love departing in later life haunts much of our literature, as in William Yeats's poem:

> When you are old and grey and full of sleep,
> And nodding by the fire, take down this book,
> And slowly read, and dream of the soft look
> Your eyes had once, and of their shadows deep . . .
>
> And bending down beside the glowing bars,
> Murmur, a little sadly, how Love fled
> And paced upon the mountains overhead
> And hid his face amid a crowd of stars.[2]

The image of Love flying away and hiding his face in the later years of our lives has formed the basis of much poetry and other literature; not just because we are mortal and hence likely to be bereaved one day but because 'old age' has been supposed to be a time of sadness when one dwells on joys that are past. It is only with the emergence of the Third Age as an acknowledged phenomenon in the last half of this century that a new genre of literature has developed, as we have already seen.

Traditional assumptions about what happens as we age are being overturned by researchers who have investigated older people's experiences, desires and expectations. In Starr and Weiner's study of eight hundred people aged sixty and over, they were asked, 'How does sex feel now compared with when you were younger?'[3] A few more women replied 'better' (41 per cent) than 'the same' (39.7 per cent). While enjoyable sex is not quite the same thing as love, most women would say that their erotic enjoyment is dependent on their loving their partner. The figures were not as satisfactory for men. A total of 35.5 per cent said it was 'worse' (compared with 19.3 per cent of women), but this was to be expected as the sexuality of men declines more sharply in later life.

Edward Brecher and his research team conducted a survey in America even larger than that of Starr and Weiner. It encompassed 1,201 wives and 1,839 husbands, aged between fifty and ninety-three years, who were asked a considerable number of questions about their happiness in marriage and their general well-being.[4] One of the objects of the study was to determine whether wives or husbands in the older age groups were happier in their marriages, for a considerable amount of radical feminist propaganda had suggested that marriage favoured the wants and needs of husbands but not those of wives. Feminists brought to public attention the existence of financially exploited and over-worked wives, women tied to their homes for long hours, emotionally and sexually frustrated wives and women bullied and even battered by their husbands. As a result one might expect that, on the whole, women would be much less happy with their marriages than their husbands. In fact, when asked to rate the happiness of their marriages 86 per cent of the wives described them as happy as against 87 per cent of the husbands; thus there was no significant difference.

When they came to look at the happiness of marriages in relation to the age of the respondents, the researchers divided them into three age groups: those in their fifties, sixties and seventies upwards. The happiness of marriages was seen to increase with age, the percentages of happy marriages being 84 per cent, 88 per cent and 91 per cent respectively. There are several reasons for this effect: first, as time went on the proportion of unhappy marriages would be culled by divorce and desertion; second, it is well known that a happy marriage makes for better health and longevity. There is, however, another possible reason for the effect: a number of the respondents reported that marriages, like good wine, improve with age. One wife, who had been married for thirty years, reported: 'My husband and I have become even more companionable and close since his retirement . . . Love gets better and sex slows down just a little bit . . . Love becomes comfortable and secure and the individuals make it as exciting as love in the earlier years.'

Additional factors may also account for the continued improvement of the quality of marriages with age. Retirement from full-time work, work that may be stressful, results in greater leisure time, which enables couples to have the time to be understanding and patient with one other. Couples may show more affection for each other when they feel the need for it themselves, as the infirmities of later life begin to impinge and they no longer have their children to turn to. As old friends die and disappear people of the same age group will inevitably draw closer together for comfort and understanding; as survivors in a rapidly changing and sometimes puzzling world.

One husband aged sixty-nine, who had been married for forty-three years and was now happy in his marriage, suggested that there were five stages of marriage: infatuation, disenchantment, misery (most divorces occur at this stage), enlightenment and love (it may take years).[5]

This may be true of some marriages, but we must expect there to be a great variety of patterns of marriage, some being successful up to middle age and then breaking down irrevocably. Many people deeply deplore the fact that of modern marriages in Western society one in three end in divorce, but we should be prepared to accept this as a social fact and recognize that the institution of marriage exists in many diverse forms in different cultures throughout the world. As our society has changed radically in many ways, so we must expect the institution to change. In modern Western society 90 per cent of us get married at some stage in our lives, and those who marry comparatively young and then divorce generally form a second and more stable marriage.

The empty nest syndrome

There used to be recognized syndrome of emotional distress and depression in women when their children left home. This was understandable in the days when most women led lives that were almost wholly devoted to their homes and the caring of children. When the mothers lost their children they forfeited their role in life and felt useless and bereaved, even though they were relieved of much of the physical work and emotional stress that child-rearing can involve. In more recent times mothers lead fuller lives with interests outside the home, even if they do not go out to work; they also have better transport than previous generations. Moreover, through the ubiquity of the telephone and other means of modern communication children who have left home can keep in touch with their parents even if they have moved far away. I know a mother in her seventies who has three daughters, all with their own families living quite long distances away, who have very substantial telephone bills because they keep in close touch, just as though they lived at the other end of the village.

Where the parents are on good terms, in place of the 'empty nest syndrome' we now have the 'empty nest honeymoon' between wives and husbands who renew their earlier affectionate closeness and enjoyment of each other's company. The 'new old' certainly have expectations for the future different from those of their predecessors. A North American joke conveys this changed attitude:

A Roman Catholic priest, a lawyer and a Rabbi were debating the question of when life can be said to begin. The priest gave his opinion that life began at the moment of conception and that it was sacred thereafter; the lawyer said that the matter was very complex legally but he would agree with whatever the Supreme Court decreed; the Rabbi said, 'Look, you guys have got it all wrong; of course life really begins when the kids leave home and the dog dies.'

While on holiday in Devon I found a tourist shop that sold car-stickers declaring 'Retired and happy spending our kids' inheritance'. My daughter did not mind it being displayed in the rear window of the car, but after a while I got tired of young people hooting at us.

Returning to Brecher's study we find a fifty-six-year-old wife who had been married for thirty-four years reporting as follows:

> Now that the children are grown and gone, we are delighted to be a single couple once again and have been on a honeymoon ever since we have been alone. We find that our shared experiences have made us closer, wiser, and funnier . . . We like being able to make love in the afternoon, if we wish, or to wait a few days longer than usual if one or another of us is not in the mood. It is a lovely time of life.[6]

In the USA, where this study was carried out, the institution of the 'retirement community' is common, but this form of association of older people is much less developed in the UK. It implies a certain level of affluence, which rules out pensioners on low incomes. It is likely that this form of community living will spread to the UK in the course of time. Such investigations as there have been have shown that there is no greater nor lesser degree of marital happiness among the couples living in such retirement communities compared with those living elsewhere whose children have left home.

Sexuality and marital relations
A proportion of older couples will have never been significantly interested in sex even when they were young, although they have

129

had quite happy marriages and perhaps been envied by friends whose marriages have been marred by emotional conflicts over sexual matters and extramarital relationships. People with a very low sex drive may even welcome the coming of the later years and the discontinuation of any sexual activity under the conventional and socially acceptable guise of 'sexless old age'. Others may cease making love simply out of boredom with what has become a fairly meaningless ritual or because one of the partners has developed a disability, such as a weak heart, which is used as an excuse for abstinence. Where the marriage has become totally sexless it may nevertheless continue quite smoothly because the partners have developed other mutual interests which bind them together. Such marriages may be somewhat vulnerable however, for by ill fortune one of the partners may meet a new acquaintance who opens up totally new and exciting vistas of experience. Older people can, and do, fall in love. They may realize that their lives have been lacking a component that they never knew existed and this may shatter a long-established marital relationship. It is safer for marriages to fulfil all sides of the nature of both partners, including the potentially erotic.

One or both members of a couple may realize the vulnerability of a marriage without sex about the time of retirement, which is a dangerous stage as they have more leisure on their hands and an uncertain future. However, one or both may say: 'For us it is too late. We might have done something about it in our younger years, but we did not. What hope is there for us now? That side of our lives is finished.' Such pessimism is often ill founded. It may not be too late, as the following case illustrates. This example was presented at the annual conference of Age Concern England in 1989:

Bob and Alice Smith looked forward to Bob's retirement with immense pleasure. He had had a boring job and longed for the time when he could spend much more of the day with Alice and look after his garden. He also wanted to help Alice because she was becoming a little bit arthritic as she got older, and he thought his contribution to the household would be very valuable to her. They had always got on well together but had not been very close emotionally.

In the last few years their sex life had deteriorated, although it had never been particularly good. This was partly because for Alice it became increasingly painful. Her vagina was dry and so penetration was not pleasant. This had a bad effect on Bob who found it more and more difficult to get an erection, although this had never troubled him when he was younger. Obviously this made the frequency of their relationship very much less and neither of them talked about this, but it added to the difficulties they experienced in their daily lives. Although they had both thought that when they retired all these problems would disappear because they would have more time to relax and enjoy life together, in fact it got worse.

Bob wanted to help Alice with the household chores but this, in fact, meant reorganizing her long-established timetable. She resented this, but did not want to hurt his feelings by making it clear. She felt he was around too much of the time getting under her feet and found it difficult to thank him for what he did. However, her resentment was fairly obvious. He found this difficult to understand and gradually became more and more withdrawn. When he made suggestions that they should go out to the seaside for the day she seemed to find excuses and insisted that she finished all the household chores before she was ready to go.

Their aggravation became intense. What had been a fairly minor problem in bed became very much worse. Even when Bob felt particularly loving and was quite sure that he would be able to perform to his own satisfaction, Alice turned over and made it quite obvious that she would not welcome his advances. On the rare occasions that Alice felt sexy and thought that she was unlikely to experience pain she found that Bob was somehow angry with her and reluctant to make love. They found their relationship becoming extremely distant and frighteningly cold.

They came to the conclusion that the only thing they could do was to separate. They went to visit their daughter and her husband to tell them that this was their decision. Their daughter was totally amazed. It had never occurred to her that things had got so bad between her parents.[7]

This is a typical case in which something that starts as a minor sexual problem ruins the whole marital relationship and causes difficulties in matters that are not related to sexuality. In a minority of women the menopause is followed by a drying up of the normal lubrication that follows sexual excitement and therefore pain is experienced on intercourse. The wife's problem then becomes the husband's as well, for the knowledge that he may hurt her causes impotence in him, even on occasions when she feels perfectly normally lubricated.

Although during the 1970s a plethora of books dealing with the sex lives of younger people was published, it has yet to be fully realized that it is not only the young who get into difficulties and need advice concerning their sexuality. Both men and women over the age of fifty may face new problems that require specialist advice. *Living, Loving and Ageing* by Wendy and Sally Greengross has much useful advice to offer.[8] They point out that nowadays GPs are perfectly willing to give advice about sexual problems to older people, who should not be shy about consulting them. In the case of Bob and Alice, if they had consulted their GP early on, some means of hormone replacement therapy might have been given to Alice and normal function restored. This form of therapy requires medical monitoring and is not always suitable, but the doctor would certainly have provided some remedy for the problem. Other books that are to be recommended in cases such as this are Alex Comfort's *A Good Age* and Butler and Lewis's *Love and Sex After Sixty*.[9, 10]

Apart from consulting books, older couples should realize that they are never too old to go for advice about their marriage to specialist counsellors available through Relate, the advisory service of the National Marriage Guidance Council. Irene Short, speaking at the Age Concern Conference, described the case of a husband aged eighty-seven and his wife aged eighty-five, married for more than sixty years, who had begun to quarrel and reckoned that their marriage was over. They attended Relate counselling sessions and after repeated visits were able to work out a solution to their disagreements. Irene Short also mentioned an elderly couple who had been married for over thirty-five years and stayed together despite the fact that their sex life had never been adequate. After a number of sessions with a Relate sex therapist over six months, they reported their 'previously disastrous' relationship had 'grown and blossomed'. It would seem that this couple had always had a distorted view of sex which had prevented them from experiencing fulfilment in love-making, but even in later life this could be rectified and their attitudes changed so that they could experience normal pleasure in it. Of their marriage they finally said that 'the first thirty-five years were the worst'.

Adultery and marriage in later life

One of the common reasons for couples splitting up is adultery followed by divorce. Divorce in the UK currently ends about one in three first marriages and has followed the trends in the USA where the rate is even higher, about 50 per cent. Of the divorced about 75 per cent remarry, generally within five years, and about 60 per cent of these remarrying divorcees remarry again. Rates in the UK have not yet caught up with US figures, but it seems likely that they will.

Most writers who focus on marriage in later life never mention this sensitive topic and one is left with the impression that older people do not commit adultery, but the facts are otherwise. It used to be that one's grandparents did not stray from the marriage bed because they were brought up in a tradition where fidelity was prized highly, but it should be remembered that those now entering the Third Age were young adults during the 'swinging sixties', when ideas about life-long monogamy underwent a radical change.

One common reason for adultery is that a partner may be afflicted by one of the ailments that become increasingly common in later life and hence be rendered uninterested in, or unfit for, love-making. Most husbands are older than their wives and in any case the sexual capacity of men declines more rapidly than that of women. In one study of 132 men and women in middle age and older who had ceased having sexual relations within marriage, it was found that by far the most common reason for such cessation was the sexual incapacity of the husband.[11]

One writer who does discuss adultery in some detail is Brecher.[12] He found that of the 1,245 wives questioned 8 per cent admitted to have engaged in adultery after the age of fifty. Although wives have obviously more reason to be unfaithful because of the growing incapacity of their husbands as they age, such is the strength of the 'double standard' regarding sex that many more of the husbands (23 per cent) admitted infidelity after the age of fifty.

An attempt was made to determine in what ways unfaithful wives differed from faithful ones in view of the great amount of information that had been gathered about these people. It was found that the strongest association was between taking a lover and a very high enjoyment of sex, which is precisely what one might expect. Faithfulness and a low level of enjoyment of sex was linked with being moderately or very religious, but, as these findings depend solely on people's self-reporting, we would hardly expect many religious people to admit to a practice that is considered taboo by their faith.

In general, those wives who remained faithful despite acknowledged temptations to do otherwise did so out of respect for the ties of marriage. One sixty-seven-year-old wife reported: 'I tried to get my husband's permission for outside sex after he could no longer function. He was shocked – and refused! I have too much respect for him, and we together have other "fun activities", so it isn't important. Our being together is important.'

A question that frequently arises is whether couples should tell one another if they are having an extramarital affair. To some people it may seem unacceptable that secrecy on such a matter should be preserved and feel it is bound to ruin the marriage eventually, but this is not always the case. A wife of seventy-five described how she and her husband both engaged in sexual adventures: 'At first we were quite frank about these, but later, realizing that it did no good to tell and that telling tended to make us insecure and jealous, we kept any such extramarital activity from each other. The extramarital experiences were good experiences and brief.' There was one exception to the brevity of such affairs, as she had started an affair with a younger man when she was aged thirty-six and this had lasted for thirty-nine years. At the time of her reporting she still had occasional sex with her sixty-eight-year-old married lover. She described her relations with her husband as 'moderately satisfactory, happy', although they no longer had sexual relations.

When one inquires into the marital relations of older couples, it becomes apparent that there is a huge variety of patterns of behaviour and it is impossible to identify a 'universal' norm or to be dogmatic about correct ways to behave. In the past there was such a blanket of silence about such matters that no one really had a clear picture of reality. While doctors, psychologists, counsellors and priests can give very useful advice to those who come to ask for it, their help is generally most effective when it is given with due regard to the mores that are observed in the particular cultural group to which patients and clients belong. Adultery appears to be so common, particularly among males, that while it is no doubt regrettable and likely to break up the marriages of some people, with others it may even render stable some marriages that would be happy if it were not for the sexual problems common in later life. Take the case of a man of seventy-two married to a woman of fifty-six: she says that they have sex a few times a month but that they do not enjoy it much. Unknown to her husband she has two lovers and reports:

> With the advent of the menopause I felt liberated, and sex can be enjoyed for the enjoyment's sake alone. My sexual regrets during my lifetime are the regrets of omission; I would have shared much more with more partners. Having no fear of pregnancy makes all the difference to me. Now sex can be spontaneous and joyous.[13]

As she is satisfied, there seems no reason why she and her husband should not continue with a marriage that may be stable although not ideal, for at their advanced ages there is no guarantee that they would form a better partnership.

Similarly a sixty-six-year-old husband writes that he and his wife have had no sex for many years:

> My marriage could have been much better, if I had known what I needed for sexual compatibility and what my intended wife needed. Despite problems we have stayed together, but we have missed much, a fact that my mistress has made abundantly clear during the years of our affair.[14]

He had a mistress aged thirty-two, the affair having started nine years earlier, but he did not wish to obtain a divorce and marry her because he felt that she would inevitably find someone more suitable and leave him. A very selfish attitude? Perhaps, but it is hard to judge whether this would not be best in the end for all three people concerned.

Brecher's study was conducted in the early 1980s across the USA, but it does not seem likely that since then any greatly significant changes have taken place or that social conditions are so very different here in the UK. Developments over the past decade or so have tended in the direction of greater equality between the sexes, with a decreasing double standard between what is acceptable behaviour for women and men. The cases cited raise more questions than easy answers, but it is only by gaining knowledge about what actually goes on in people's marriages that individuals, couples and their advisers can arrive at better solutions to the problems that arise.

Part 2

Cecily
'Just a beginner'

Finally, at the age of sixty-one, I'd reached a plateau of solitary, quiet, satisfying living: no job, no husband, no children and no demands; blissfully unstressed. I had staunch women friends who were stimulating company, my own small house and independent income and, above all, affectionate children and grandchildren.

The city where I lived provided a wealth of opportunities in the form of new interests, satisfying voluntary work, old passions and new acquaintances. All kinds of holidays were open to me. It was now myself who made important decisions that needed no explanation, and I could do exactly as I liked when I liked, without having to persuade, gratify or mollify a single soul. It was delightful to read books with my meals, eat at any time or skip eating altogether, even eat in the street; go to pubs on my own, be solitary when I felt like it; for I was unknown in the city, a nobody, and that had many compensations.

Yet I missed the company of men – their conversation and disparate attitudes to events and affairs. Talking with my women friends in the same situation, we agreed that although we mixed with some married friends, male relatives and kindly sons-in-law and had done all we could to make our lives satisfying, there was a gap in our lives as far as the company of men was concerned for, with the passing of years, our generation of men steadily dwindled in number.

We had dealt with the emotional emptiness of living on one's own for oneself: the outlet for love and affection limited to our family and friends, whatever degree of success we'd had as wives, mothers and home-makers. However, I became more and more acutely conscious of couples everywhere, especially those of my own age, strolling arm in arm by the river, holding hands in the theatre. It made me feel wistful yet cheered and encouraged that some marriages had successfully survived the ruck of everyday living, the partial erosion that is family life.

Arising in the morning and opening my window I'd watch groups of young men with sun-browned arms and legs jogging in packs past my garden, and I'd think: They have no idea an ageing woman is watching them, harmlessly enjoying their display of youthful vigour and high spirits. Elderly women are not expected to show such interest, but I felt better and hopeful because of them. They cheered me, and I was glad they ran by as they did, often joyfully shouting in sun or rain.

Yet no thought of any relationship with a man other than friendship, mutually agreeable, even perhaps practical, had entered my head. Indeed, in a routine interview with my doctor, I was utterly amazed at the matter-of-fact questions about my sex life, both after a smear test and during an appointment over an orthopaedic problem. I laughed I was so astonished and joked about it with my women friends, who were equally amused.

However, I was surprised at my reaction when a male colleague gave me a hug in return for a birthday bottle of wine. I felt I wanted to rest my head on his shoulder for longer than the brief couple of seconds that I had.

One day, I heard from a mutual acquaintance about a man who had once been her neighbour, living on his own in a nearby street. She was concerned about him after his wife's death some time before. He seemed emotionally awry: an aloof man, sad and lost. I though this would be a chance to make a male friend and used to look out for him as I passed his door or met at a club to which we both belonged. I made most of the running in conversation as he was very shy. Verbal exchanges blossomed into meetings, invitations to parties, sorties of all kinds, as well as evenings together in each other's house. It was immensely enjoyable and very exciting to look forward to meetings, getting ready to go out, anticipating great pleasure in just each other's company: a revival of the joys of being young, carefree and single but with much more experience!

All this time we kept a distance between us, both physical and emotional. He was considerably older, our backgrounds were very different and his marriage had been a long and happy one, despite other women on its periphery. Although shy, he was absolutely frank, answering my searching questions fully about this situation: questions naturally stemming from my own experience in marriage.

This had lasted over thirty years and had initially been a very happy one, despite the fact that my husband was a consistent philanderer. Otherwise a good husband and father, he had helped me build a close and affectionate family framework that firmly bonded us together. The later half of the marriage considerably deteriorated, partly owing to the change in the locality and nature of his job and our home. This fanned the instability in my husband's nature and made him behave in an increasingly unreasonable and erratic manner, often causing suffering not only on my part but also to our children, now in their teens. Not only were there successive, or even concurrent, mistresses but the guilt engendered by his defection and emotional neglect made him sometimes both vicious and outrageously unkind and self-centred.

I clung on to the marriage, hoping that early retirement, the departure of children from home, a change of surroundings would improve matters. It was not to be. The advent of yet another young mistress and a serious operation for me brought an unbearable situation to an explosive climax. I packed within an hour and left my home behind me.

The next few years were traumatic with the strains of rootlessness, finding a job, searching for and buying a house (I began to appreciate some of the frustrations that had sparked off the feminist movement). Added to these was the turmoil of a long-drawn-out divorce: a juggernaut process. These experiences exhausted me emotionally with their wild swings of hope and despair. The sheer challenge of surviving with ever-narrowing horizons mopped up most of my energy.

Time passed. Time healed. I reached the point at which my tale begins and on to where I had made a friend of a man, assuming that nothing more than that was possible or necessary. Despite great differences of opinion on many topics, we had many interests in common, and both drew strength and enjoyment from our relationship. I felt really happy after so many years.

I was immensely shy, partly by nature and partly through lack of confidence engendered by the failure of my marriage. Divorce had left me feeling that no man would be interested in what I was or did. My ex-husband's consistent need to seek outside the marriage was evidence of my lack of attraction – and now I was even older.

Gradually, the beneficence of my friend's affection and care warmed my feelings: he brought me flowers, offered me compliments and little courtesies; he also came up with schemes to enhance my happiness and generally expressed care and concern. Then came, with other contrivances, hints at another kind of relationship, for he had respected my nervous detachment and caution with patience, tact and sensitivity.

An enforced parting by way of a family holiday, through exchange of letters, brought matters to a head as he wrote of the possibility of more than platonic friendship, quoting Donne's

'Love's mysteries in souls do grow/ But yet the body is his book'
and 'Else a great prince in prison lies'. My reaction was to write
of the absurdity, the utter grotesqueness of elderly physical love
expressed with wrinkled, patchy skin, flabby, fat, scarred bodies,
bald head, dim eyes, dry, thin hair, stained or artificial teeth. It
was bizarre, yet I had to remind myself that not all young and
middle-aged people are handsome or beautiful.

Tremors of expectations remained, for I was aware that right at
the beginning there had been a frisson between us and that his
presence disturbed me, his touch even more, so that I avoided
looking him in the eye for a great deal of the time. I was utterly
amazed that my knees began to turn to water and my body to
respond in a way that I would not have believed possible for a
woman in her sixties. What was happening to me? Could he be
aware of what I was feeling, with his wide experience of women?

Inevitably one evening we held hands; he held me closely and
kissed me warmly. Soon after when he came to my house I took
his hand and said simply, 'What would you say if I invited you to
come to bed with me?' With an exhilarating mixture of excitement and apprehension fermenting inside me, I led us upstairs. I
was terrified and achingly curious as I'd not slept with anyone for
seven years.

I need not have worried. In my single bed he held me close and
reassured me, stroking me lovingly and whispering tender
endearments, nullifying my expressed inadequacies over the
defects of my body, my dereliction in the arts of love. I flowed
with the release, the relief from tension in response to the passion
of his love-making. It is difficult to put into words the marvel of
loving consummation in old age: the warmth, the glow, the gen-
tleness from mutual consideration, the actuality of loving arms
enfolding one away from a menacing or indifferent world; to be
succoured by embraces and loving kindness at a time when one
is vividly aware of the inevitable invasion by infirmity and death.

All I can express is the unutterable delight of that night in particular for the joy and the glow was such that when I woke on my own in the morning, blissfully relaxed and inspired, I did not want to move and break the spell, for I knew it to be a unique experience. I lay motionless for a long time savouring the fervour, the luminosity within me which I knew could never be quite the same again.

Since that time there have been many similar occasions. There is a very special quality to love-making at my age. It is unlike that of youth or middle age in its flowering of tender consideration for the other person, its manifestations of gratitude rather than gratification and truly affectionate passion, and I count myself fortunate in having a sensitive and skilful lover.

Lover, for we have not married nor shall we marry. We retain our independence and live in separate houses, yet I do not know what I would do without him, and if we have the slightest quarrel I am miserable until we have quite made it up. Such occasions are fortunately rare, but they serve to remind one that we are, in fact, 'in love'.

Of course one day one of us will have to be on our own again, and he is older than I am. He is a complete unbeliever who laughs at the idea of an afterlife, but he jokes about waiting there on the banks of the River Styx until I arrive and we cross together in Charon's ferry-boat. Fortunately we are both in pretty good health and so we do not really think of death. We live in the present and life is most rewarding and enjoyable with much laughter. What one really fears is not death but sinking into decrepitude. What will we do if one of us becomes feeble and helpless? So we wish for each other a sudden and unexpected death in the midst of a busy and active life: it is what we both want.

Postscript
Since this affair started I have learned that it is not so unusual for

women to form passionate attachments in later, often very late, life. It has been an absolute revelation to me that I am not odd and eccentric. Much more information is being made available to women on this theme, and I am glad because it is such a joyous, happy and very special experience. I hope that others will take heart from my story and will become just a beginner, like me.

Commentary

Cicely gives her account the title 'Just a beginner'. She is a woman in her sixties who has led a fairly conventional life, having been a virtuous wife for over thirty years and having reared three children. Her marriage ended in divorce in her fifties when she left her husband whose behaviour had become increasingly intolerable. There must be many women in her position, divorcees or widows who have settled down as single women and who are enjoying their new-found independence with plenty of friends and no lack of occupations and interest.

Being a fairly conventional woman, Cicely took it for granted that she would remain celibate for the rest of her life and, indeed, she was very surprised when her doctor inquired about her sex life. She relates how she regarded it as 'bizarre' that anyone should consider that she might form a new erotic relationship at her age, with her wrinkles and other marks of age. Being a normal woman, she appreciated a new friendship with a compatible man and was then astonished to find that she was falling in love with him, with all the attendant physical symptoms that she had not experienced since she was a young woman. She writes, 'I was utterly amazed that my knees began to turn to water and my body to respond in a way I would not have believed possible for a woman in her sixties.' She has realized that she was quite wrong in her expectations of what life would be like in her years of retirement and that she is indeed 'just a beginner'.

What is significant about her experience is that she does not intend to marry her lover. She has tasted the freedom of being a single woman for several years, and as social mores have become more liberal she finds it quite possible to enjoy all the pleasures of a stable erotic relationship, to give and receive love of considerable warmth, yet retain the independence and freedom of living alone in her own house, although with the frequent company of her lover. This theme is repeated a number of times in the accounts that follow.

Gertrude
'His children were hostile'

When we first met I was fifty and he was a widower of sixty, his wife having died after a long illness a few months earlier. I had never been married, and the thought of doing so had never entered my head, as I had led a very busy and interesting life. I had a good job in local government and was in the process of buying my own house.

We were complete opposites in many ways: I was used to city life and he was country born and bred; all my relations had died, but he had lots as well as grown-up children. On top of this we had only briefly corresponded before deciding to meet, so it was with some trepidation that I looked forward to our first meeting. He duly arrived late one Saturday morning after quite a long journey. How vividly I remember that occasion. It was love at first sight, something I had never believed in, but it was just as though we had known each other all our lives. After a wonderful weekend together we became engaged on the Tuesday and were married a very few weeks later.

Not unnaturally my close friends were horrified and, as far as they were concerned, our marriage was doomed to failure. How could I have been so foolish? they asked. One of their predictions, however, proved to be true.

It was on our wedding day that I first met my husband's children and immediately an awful feeling of doom swept over me; the unspoken hostility was obvious to both of us. As they were all grown up, happily married with children of their own we had not

149

expected such a violent reaction. We had thought that they would have been glad to shed the responsibility of a parent living alone. How wrong we were. Of course we had both realized that it would take a little time for us all to adjust and gradually get to know one another. We were quite prepared for that, but his children really did not seem to want to see their father happy again. Their anger was all directed against him and was nothing to do with me. It was their way of punishing him for what they considered disrespect towards their mother.

I had undertaken quite a lot of counselling work outside my normal job, so I decided to talk to each of them individually, but it was hopeless and I quickly realized that only time could heal and that we must plan our life without, or with very little, contact. It was very different from what we had both expected.

In spite of everything we had fifteen wonderful years together. He infected me with his keen interest in all kinds of sports. He introduced me to boats, caravans and fishing and he always wanted me to succeed in all our activities, insisting that I had the very best equipment, and he was a patient and skilful teacher.

To ease him into retirement we bought a fairly dilapidated cottage on the coast. It needed a good deal doing to it and we decided to undertake the restoration ourselves. It was very hard work but great fun, and the satisfaction of seeing one job after another completed was significant. I would not have believed that anyone would have got me on to a roof handling tiles, but he did, and by the time the roof was finished I was walking about on those narrow strips of timber as though I had been doing it for years and loving every moment. The view out to sea was terrific – in contrast to the wilderness of the garden below awaiting our attention. I also helped mix concrete for the paths, helped erect the garage and install central heating. He gave me so many interests and new skills.

Later on when all the work was done and the garden established he found equal pleasure in helping me indoors with deep-freezing fresh produce and the fish we caught. He also became interested in cooking; life was full of fun. If only his family had joined in our happiness would have been complete, but alas the barrier remained. They set out to hurt him and they succeeded.

Our relationship ended as suddenly as it commenced. We never said goodbye. It still deeply hurts me to think that he died alone outside. Apparently he had a heart attack. I know I couldn't have done anything, but I would have liked to have been with him.

I did not experience love in early life, but nothing could have been better than this late relationship that showed me clearly that love is about sharing and giving, about someone else's happiness being more important than one's own. I was asked the other day if I would ever marry again, and I had no hesitation in saying yes. Living alone is an empty existence. I am sure that we are meant to share the love each of us possesses. Age is immaterial.

Commentary

It seems likely that Gertrude met her husband through a dating agency which arranged for them to correspond and then meet. She does not tell us why at the age of fifty she decided to marry for the first time; she writes that previously the thought of marriage had never entered her head. I did not pursue this matter with her, as I felt that one of the most significant aspects of her account was that, to the surprise of both her and her husband, his children remained hostile to their father's remarriage.

The hostility of children to a parent's remarriage is by no means uncommon. Gertrude attributed the hostility of her stepchildren to a wish to punish their father for being disrespectful to their late mother. This is possible, for some children will enshrine the memory of a dead parent, although such an ostensible reason may be a cover for less admirable motives. It is known that where sons and daughters are unhappily single or in unsatisfactory marriages they may demonstrate jealousy of a parent whom they had considered 'past it'. Gertrude, however, says that her stepchildren were 'happily married'. I wonder whether this was in fact the case, for it is very difficult to ascertain that people's marriages are satisfactory. As she relates, she tried to talk individually to her husband's children but without much effect and without managing to establish for certain the true reason for their hostility.

After writing this account of her marriage Gertrude later wrote to me, 'Since my husband died I have managed to establish a kind of relationship with his children and I do hear from them and see them occasionally. In some strange way this in itself hurts, because it was the relationship between him and them that mattered, not between them and me.'

We shall never know the reasons why the children in this case became unrelentingly hostile to their father after his remarriage, but those who have had a similar experience when they have formed a new love relationship in later life may take comfort in the fact that time may eventually heal such a breach.

This account highlights the risk people in later life run if they form a new relationship because of the increased probability that it will be terminated relatively quickly by the death of their partner. Gertrude's happy marriage was ended quite suddenly by her husand's fatal heart attack. Although obviously deeply grieved by her bereavement, she makes it clear not only that she thought the marriage had been worth while but, like the Wife of Bath, she would be ready to marry again.

Harriet
'Marie and I would be lost
without each other'

My partner and I arrived in the South of France unknown to each other, she a year before me with her husband who was ill. He died not long after. I was sixty-two at the time and she was fifty-three.

I arrived and settled down in a nearby village and occupied myself with gardening, as the house was only three years old and, being built on an old vineyard, there was much work to be done. I needed social outlets and so I helped with the grape harvest and joined in village activities, but my lack of French hindered me. I decided to go to church on Sundays as much for a social activity as to see if there was anything religious for me in it. At first I attended the church in the main town, but I disliked the formality there, so I went to the small church in the next village where my partner (whom I shall call Marie) had rented a house with her husband.

After he died she bought a plot of land and began clearing it of weeds and brambles to occupy herself and get her through the first year of bereavement. She was looking around for a friend to share walks with and other activities but said later that she had found no one suitable. Like me, she wandered into the local church to see what she could find. This may sound irreverent, but neither of us were enamoured with organized forms of religion. I stood in the row at the back trying to look inconspicuous and in she came, rather late. It was winter and extremely cold and everyone had hats and coats on, so we could see little of one another's face. I immediately felt some sort of silent communication between us;

she apparently wondered who I was and grew curious. It was inevitable that we should attempt to find out as much as possible about one other, and we got ourselves introduced.

At first the friendship was slow to develop. Marie went away on holiday and I lost touch and was surprised to find how lonely I felt. She returned, unknown to me, and turned up one day at my house. I was cleaning out the garage and looked a mess, but she seemed amused. We stopped for tea. That was how it was for a month or so. She would arrived unannounced, have tea and then suddenly get up and go. I later learned that this was a behaviour pattern natural to her, but at first it bothered me as I wanted her to stay longer, but I was very tongue-tied – just like a teenager. I was not at this point aware of my feelings and neither was she.

One morning I woke up to a beautiful sunny day and decided to go for a walk. I phoned her and suggested that she come with me, and she was delighted. I felt like sixteen years old that day. Our picnic was heaven, I felt energetic and lively and all the birds seemed to be singing, but still neither of us was aware of our feelings. After a few weeks of walking and having meals together, one day it dawned on me that I had fallen in love.

It was a bombshell. Did she care for me? Was she interested? I remember the agony of the months in between then and when we really got together. The pain of love in youth is no different from when we get older. My head spun. I drove past her house whenever I could and told myself that I was being ridiculous. When I saw her my heart leaped. Finally one day, while sitting on the settee in her house having tea, she kissed me and the world turned upside down.

I was still married, although only in name, and my family was living in England. I was not looking for anyone. The idea had not entered my head, although I found that I was drawn to Marie in some inexplicable way. When I did recognize my feelings I was as helpless as when I was young and in love; it was no different. Still, it was good to feel so young and healthy again.   It hit her all of a sudden too, and now we meet each other every day. We have found that we have much in common: hobbies, habits, likes and dislikes. We are both strong characters neither of whom says 'yes, dear' to the other, and are aware that we could quarrel bitterly. But we do not want to argue and are able to discuss our differences, even if it gets a bit heated sometimes. And it is good making up afterwards.

Marie is different from me in that she has had only one marriage and lover and never thought about having a relationship with a woman. I, on the other hand, have been married twice and had many relationships with men. In my younger days I also had a couple of love friendships with women, but neither of these was truly sexual. It was not until I recognized my feelings for Marie that I knew that I could have a proper sexual relationship with a woman. It seemed strange to me at first that a sixty-two-year-old and a fifty-three-year-old were jumping into bed with each other like teenagers, but now I accept this age leap backwards was part of the excitement. We both feel young, cared for and wanted. Loneliness has disappeared and we have purpose in our lives. When we see some of our neighbours milling around in a lost sort of way it is sad, and we reflect on how lucky we are to have each other. My old friends say how much I have changed, how young I look and how happy I seem. Some of them know why but not all of them, as I do not feel I can tell everyone. Marie's family seem pleased that she has a friend who has a lot in common with her and I get on with all of them.

At first our love was exciting and thrilling, then it gradually changed to a deeper, caring love. Although the initial stages of our relationship were stimulating, I find the deeper love that has developed more satisfying and stable. Still, when I see her unexpectedly my heart misses a beat and when we are apart for a few days it is unbearable for both of us, and we are aware of the strong links between us. Neither knows what lies in the future, but we feel that we shall be together one day, even though we are not yet ready for a complete sharing of our lives, as we both jealously guard our privacy.

I know that all this could end for a variety of reasons, just as relationships did when I was young, and I also know that I would be devastated and heartbroken, but it will have been a worthwhile experience. I would never say no to love. It is so precious that I think that we should open ourselves up to it wherever we find it, no matter what the source. Somehow we expand with love and life seems more possible. I know that Marie feels the same, and we would be lost without each other.

Commentary

This is an account of a lesbian relationship formed by a woman in her early sixties who had previously been married twice and had a family. She was separated from her husband and says that she was not looking for a new relationship. Not only had she been married, but she admits to having had various affairs with men when younger and two 'love friendships' with women, but the latter are described as not being 'truly sexual', unlike her present relationship.

Like Cecily, Harriet was astonished to find herself falling in love at her age and the affair reminded her of her feelings when she was very young. Her surprise that age makes no difference to the forming of a new relationship is by no means unique in people of her generation or older. Our society has influenced people to think that they will lose the capacity for erotic love in later life and the reality surprises them.

The fact that this is an account of the formation of a lesbian relationship makes little difference. All that is written by Harriet might just as well have been written of a heterosexual relationship. There are now many more women than men in this age group and it will be impossible for a great number of older women to find male partners at this stage in their life. Some serious writers have suggested alternative solutions: one is a form of polygamy – which may not commend itself to many women – and another is lesbianism. The feminist movement has made lesbianism quite respectable in the eyes of many people and Harriet's story shows how a woman who has been heterosexual in her younger years may find fulfilment in erotic love in her later years with someone of her own sex.

Susie
'Friends warned me about the age gap'

As I crossed the crowded saloon bar to reach the children in the pub garden, there he was, wild, animated, bearded and magnetic. I made a detour so that I could walk through his group of admiring friends, apologizing as I went.

'Who are you, hen, and what are you drinking?' he said in a rough Scottish voice. I'd done it; he'd noticed me.

This was to be the beginning of seven kaleidoscopic years with a man thirty years older than me. Mario was fifty-nine when we met and I was twenty-nine. Friends warned me of the pitfalls of such an age gap. My family pretended it wasn't happening, and neither welcomed nor mentioned him. My husband had drowned two years earlier when my daughter was two months old and my son was two years old, and I was just beginning to acknowledge my sexual needs again. My children adored my new lover and his free and easy lifestyle and I adored him too. Life was passionate again, and I felt cherished and secure once more.

All was not plain sailing: he could be quite violent when drunk, and he drank often, but I quickly learned how to manage his moods when he had been drinking and how to guide him along more peaceful paths.

I moved into his bohemian life almost immediately and felt that I had come home. His little house had murals and graffiti on the walls, mostly of a radical political nature, and the children were encouraged to express themselves in paint and crayon on any wall they chose. They found this amazingly naughty and boasted about it when visiting my mother. This gave her added grounds for criticism: did I want anti-social children? His bookshelves were full of books by authors such as Proudhon and Kropotkin, and his political views and actions added to the attraction I already felt for him – and to the excitement.

He was a professional artist, although his lack of confidence and loathing of art gallery owners and the pretentions of the art world limited his success as a painter.

Three months after we moved in together we had the chance of a bargain package holiday to Ibiza. We went for a week and stayed for a year and a half. Our time there was idyllic. Away from the reproachfulness and amusement of others, we spent lazy, sunny days, swimming, eating and socializing. He seemed to attract all the hippies on the island, and our farmhouse often overflowed with visitors. He painted local scenes and sold them to tourists for small amounts of money. His philosophy was that you charged according to your needs and wine was cheap. I rather regretted parting with his charming paintings for so little reward, but he was happy with the arrangement and that was all that mattered. I was living on a widow's pension and supplemented our income by singing in bars and clubs from time to time.

He told stories so vividly that to this day I often cannot remember whether I actually witnessed an event or whether his verbal account made me feel I'd been present. He was a vibrant and considerate lover and took great pleasure in giving pleasure. He had the gift of making me feel glamorous and feel proud of my body and he obviously loved my ample build which had always been an embarrassment to me. For the first time I became confident and adventurous in bed.

I would forgive him everything several times a week and he would promise never to upset me again, so life consisted of a series of fiery arguments and tender reconciliations. It must sound like a terribly draining existence, and so it was, but we seemed to thrive on it, and the children – now adults – are amazingly well-adjusted people and the envy of my friends. They seem to have a compassion for people which is unusual in the young.

I used to tease Mario about his deep sense of remorse and tell him that his *mea culpa* attitude was due to his Italian Catholic upbringing. He refused to admit the influence that Catholicism had had on his life, but as a lapsed Catholic myself I knew. So confession and forgiveness formed the hub of our relationship. On one occasion a favourite captain's chair of mine disappeared from the living room. He claimed to know nothing about this. A week later a similar chair reappeared and with it the 'confession'. He had had the chance to buy some duty-free whisky and had sold the chair to pay for it. The drink-worn grey-bearded patriarch managed to look about seven years old on these occasions.

Towards the end of the affair I began to notice what everyone else had always seen in neon lights. I can remember when it happened, and I am not proud to recount it here.

I woke up one morning to see him standing naked by an open window and in the pale sunlight I could see the skin on his upper arms wrinkling down over his elbows. I knew that he had begun to turn the corner into old age. I knew that I could not accompany him around this corner. The break-up was slow and painful. I felt that I had robbed him of a chance of companionship in his old age; he felt that he had robbed me of my youth. Now, fifteen years later, I doubt I would have been affected by something as trivial as an ageing body. The children were upset by the separation and seemed to blame me for it, even though his behaviour in general was far more reprehensible than mine.

We continued to remain friends, and he was always sensitive to my new situations and never encroached on my new relationships if he approved of the man in question. I always felt that he was monitoring my progress in a non-possessive yet protective way. Five years ago, when he was seventy, he moved into a small flat and I helped him settle in, aware of the wrench it had been for him to leave his shabby prefab vibrant with memories. It was a charming, nostalgic day spent sorting through old photographs, books and letters, and in the early evening we fell into bed together just because it seemed right. I have had many lovers, but never before or since have I experienced such passionate and compassionate love-making. We laughed, cried and clung to each other as though our lives depended on it. We were to make love from time to time over the next five years, but his worsening emphysema took much of the passion out of it, and our afternoons in bed became more an extension of our affection for each other than anything lustful.

He died two days before his seventy-fifth birthday and I was devastated. I felt that I had lost a friend, lover, protector and soul mate. I now feel quite vulnerable, even though I am in a well-established relationship. There is no longer anyone out there looking out for me, forgiving me in advance, for anything I do. No one before or since has made me feel so cherished, valued and unique. My father died when I was sixteen and, while he was very different from my lover in personality, they shared a compassion for people and acceptance of their shortcomings. I had been living a life so contrary to the one expected of me by my parents that perhaps I always felt guilty for not having the conventional lifestyle enjoyed by my sister.

And what did I mean to him? Friends tell me that he adored me, that even in his worst drunken states his passion for me was evident. He was jealous of my friendships with younger men and convinced that I was having a series of affairs. But often he would encourage me to take a younger lover, although I never needed to do this until late in the affair. My greatest regret is that he never found a partner after we parted. Yet I find comfort in the knowledge that he knew that I was always in reach if he needed me. My life and that of my children would have lacked lustre without him, and we cherish our memories of this true bohemian whose bark was far worse than his bite.

Commentary

This is an account of a woman who formed a love relationship with a man thirty years her senior. After living with him for seven years the young woman perceives that he has 'begun to turn the corner into old age' and feels that she must leave him. She continues to love him until he dies, but it is obvious from her account that as he became increasingly inadequate sexually (and this was hastened by his heavy drinking and emphysema) the glamour that once surrounded him began to fade and she felt that she needed to find a younger man. Had they been a conventional couple and had she been his wife, they might have stayed together for form's sake, but as their lifestyle was bohemian the break occurred and he became a father figure to her. The ending of their relationship is sad, but one feels that both of them got something very positive out of it. He was a very difficult man to live with and a more mature woman might not have tolerated him for so long.

Monica
'A friendship between opposites'

In discussing my relationships, I find myself inhibited by two considerations. The first is that among the several recent associations I have experienced few could be described as 'love'. Love implies a romantic passion of the sort we rarely feel in later years and, although one can cite satisfactory marriages between elderly people, they are often more marriages of sense and suitability than anything as powerful as love. Of course I am being subjective in assuming that relationships must be heterosexual, as the word 'love' covers a range of experiences.

The second inhibiting consideration is that total honesty is a near impossibility, particularly when touching anything of a sexual character. We all have our self-deceptions, pretences or minor hypocrisies which vary with our backgrounds and upbringings. Often men will pretend to have been rakes when they have not been and women of my age group may present an image of themselves as more devoted, monogamous wives than they actually are and claim that their husband is 'the only man I ever really cared about'. My generation was brought up to maintain certain false delicacies in matters of truth and etiquette. We are now in the 1990s. We have had the supposed sexual revolution of the 1960s, Germaine Greer, the Pill and Women's Liberation, all of which encouraged us to talk and think more honestly about ourselves. These days women tend not to project romanticized images of themselves, and we are discouraged from sentimentality by those honest women novelists who are frank about the feelings of those in their age group. Iris Murdoch, sometimes allegorical, always truthful, says that anyone claiming to have been blissfully married for many years is, at least, a self-deceiver if not a positive liar.

I think it was George Bernard Shaw who said that friends never become lovers but that lovers sometimes become friends. Such was the case in the account of my association with a widower neighbour whom I met some three years ago, following the move to a smaller house after the death of my husband.

We were both grieving the deaths of our partners; both considering ourselves to have been happily married for some forty years. Peter had nursed his wife through a long, painful illness, whereas I had been spared the misery of watching a loved one suffer, because my husband died in his sleep without a day's illness 'at the end of a perfect day'.

Peter contrasts in every way with my husband. Peter's was a crowded household with two daughters, each with a child living under the same roof. One daughter had returned from abroad in order to help with nursing her loved mother and the other was divorced from her husband. Peter deplored the disorder of his household and his comment on his only grandson was 'I don't much like him and he doesn't like me.' One blessing of a sudden death, such as I experienced, is that those left are so benumbed by shock that they don't absorb the full horror. But by the time I moved here the numbness had been replaced by emptiness and a 'left-over life to kill' feeling.

When I was moderately settled in I gave a small drinks party for those of my old neighbours who had not seen my new house, among them a jolly spinster from the village with whom I had long been on friendly terms. After the party she walked around the corner to have Sunday lunch with her brother-in-law Peter and his family, who were now all that remained of her family. Later she insisted that he invite his new neighbours to a dinner party. And so we met and there rapidly developed an affair – for want of a better word – which met with the immediate approval of our families, all of whom were glad to have us diverted.

It may surprise those of my generation who believe that women over fifty years are immune to physical attraction, but I must confess that my initial interest in Peter was a physical one. He was tall and fairish and had been fortunate in retaining a slim figure and thick hair. He was retired from the Royal Air Force and I could see from a photograph of him with his bomber wartime command crew that he had been a dashing young fellow. Other guests at our first dinner together were two retired Air Force couples who seemed to share a raffish camaraderie with Peter and who fascinated me with their racy tales of service experience.

Whatever the chemistry in those early days, I think the attraction was a one-sided one. His down-to-earth explanation was to term it 'sex starvation', as his first impression of me was that I was 'a poor old thing who was well past it'. In fact, it did not take long for him to find out that I was not, but the extraordinary nature of his marriage made me think that he had been conditioned into being 'past it' of necessity.

His marriage was happy in every area except that of sex, which his wife positively disliked. She would only allow him near her once a month, and then it was more of a duty than a pleasure. He remained faithful to her throughout their marriage, and I believe it says much of his devotion or strength of character that a normally if not highly sexed man should have resisted the temptation to seek comfort elsewhere.

He told me of his randy young days when airmen packed in all the wine, women and song they could find, because they truly believed every mission would be their last. He had once escaped death by being admitted to hospital before a bombing raid from which his entire crew failed to return. I listened alarmed to stories of his and his colleagues' exploits. 'Listen' is the operative

165

word, as he is an endless talker and a poor listener, as are all his family.

Now I can scarcely remember how our first meeting developed so fast into an intimate companionship where we were together much of the time. My sardonic elder son thought I would quickly become bored, but I explained that at my age one does not give up a workable friendship because of a little boredom. Is it not tacitly understood that the best of friends bore one another occasionally? I often feel exasperated by Peter's inability to listen and sometimes by his mundane, egocentric conversations, though just when I feel I can listen no longer he amuses me with a flash of humorous self-mockery.

Long ago I heard it said that one is neither as happy or as miserable as one thinks, a statement my late husband regarded as a negative one. His view makes me think that I am exaggerating when I say how fortunate I felt for the next two years, often believing myself so happy that I knew it could not last.

Before I go into detail about what brought the good days to an end, I must dwell on the pleasures of those two years. It was lovely to have lonely evenings occupied again and to have a personable male escort, to say nothing of the practical advantage of a willing, unpaid handyman. It was an agreeable surprise that Peter was accepted by those friends who had expressed a wish to meet him; a request I thought was prurient, but they appeared to have a genuine liking, especially the women! We were invited to dinner parties, we entertained, and I dragged him to all manner of events he would never have dreamed of attending. For instance, we went to see a stage production of Congreve's *The Way of the World*. He was polite enough about it but could not see why his sister-in-law and I should find it so funny.

Peter is the owner of a two-bedroom bungalow in a lovely part of Provence and, when we scarcely knew one another, he alarmed me by suggesting that we should go there so that he could accomplish a few repairs and while away a few dreary winter weeks. It had been his family's holiday home for twenty years or so, when his wife, without a word of French, had purchased a plot of land on a mountainside overlooking the sea. Together they had created an attractive retreat out of a muddy patch, she being a gifted gardener and he a talented handyman. When I was finally persuaded to go there I was glad. The garden especially was a delight. There was a circle of terracotta tiles – meticulously laid out by Peter – surrounded by a shady border of roses, flowers and shrubs, a fig tree and an apple tree, also a pergola from which tumbled luxurious blossoms where it was a joy to sit in the cool evening breezes. In the heat of the day we lounged and ate on a covered porch where a passion flower almost covered the wire netting.

I found increasing enjoyment in our French holidays. My younger son worked in Milan and was thankful to have a break from the rigours of journalism by buying a return ticket to Toulon and spending a lazy weekend with us. He and Peter strongly approved of one another. The approval between my elder son and Peter was markedly less pronounced. My only daughter described him as 'not bad' and referred to him as my 'gentleman friend'. Kind though he could be, he was only occasionally polite and regarded my social niceties as hypocrisy.

Our lives changed suddenly and dramatically last November when Peter had a mild stroke. Fortunately it was only mild. I was with him at the time so was able to call a doctor who considered there was nothing that could be done beyond giving Peter a few weeks of patient nursing. By this time his daughters had moved into council houses near by, so he was enjoying the peace and order of a house to himself. Between us, with the aid of nurses and physiotherapists, we managed to nurse him through some distressing weeks. It was sad to see a once fit man laid low so suddenly. His tough RAF training compelled him to exercise when he might have better rested; consequently, he fell and broke some ribs. Nevertheless he progressed fairly well until his excellent doctor suspected that he had an aortic aneurysm, which would require major surgery.

He had three operations in all, and his daughters were twice called to the hospital as he was expected to die. Thankfully he improved gradually, so that in a few weeks he was his usual complaining self – the hospital was a hell-hole, the nurses were all bitches, the doctors all idiots, fellow patients unbearable and the throngs of visitors and children who came to see them were noisy and stupid. It was no surprise when Peter more or less removed himself from hospital and it must have been an almighty relief to the staff. There followed weeks when life seemed a long, dark tunnel with only a glimmer at the end. Only now does he begin to lead a more normal life, although whether he will ever make the adjustment to some degree of incapacity remains to be seen. His difficulty is that of a practical man who has hardly read a book in his life. In vain have I tried to introduce him to books he might like, but he returns them hastily and remains baffled that anyone 'can see anything in them'.

What remains now is to thank the gods that he seems to be recovering and to consider those positives that developed from an initially negative companionship of convenience.

John Steinbeck said that women value laughter more than love, and I wonder if one is possible without the other. I laugh both at and with Peter. Laughter is the constant positive: 'with' because his humour is unfailing and 'at' because he is so awful. Wendy Cope said that there are so many kinds of awful men and he certainly has one kind of awfulness I never encountered before. So our friendship is educative, as I am beginning to learn more about the seamy side of life and those creatures I never before knew existed. He evidently finds me as strange as I find him, since he enjoys mocking me and derides my ignorance of such vitals as the internal combustion engine, finance and politics. It is a friendship between opposites who have few tastes in common, not even in food. He is a man with few affections apart from machines, dogs and his two ancient cats, animals being the only live creatures for whom he actually demonstrates affection. His relations consider that he has improved in more than health, although I shall never be clear whether he has or whether I am merely getting used to him.

My conclusion is that we cannot afford to deny love in later life, whatever its imperfections. It may be of a kind we should never have considered in earlier, more idealistic days, but now we must enjoy what we may while we may.

Commentary

This is an account of a woman and a man who formed a stable relationship in later life despite the fact that in many important ways they appear to have been utterly unsuited to one other. She is a cultured middle-class woman with literary interests and he a man whom she describes as having 'hardly read a book in his life' and outrageously 'philistine' in his outlook and behaviour. Their initial association was due mainly to sexual attraction, she taking the lead in this matter, although he declared that in his initial opinion she was 'a poor old thing who was well past it', an impression that she was soon to dispel. She appears to have been considerably more sophisticated sexually than he.

Monica begins her account by questioning whether her association with her friend Peter can be called 'love' and refers to 'those positives that developed from an initially negative companionship of convenience'. He is described as being 'awful'. I found her account very moving because, after two years of enjoyable association with him, he became very ill and for a long period she was no longer his lover in a sexual sense but his nurse, putting up with this irascible, boorish man who never showed affection for any creatures apart from dogs and cats. She is puzzled about her feelings for him, but an observer might say that she is demonstrating a tender and compassionate love.

It is interesting that she expresses the sentiments about love in words almost identical to those used by Harriet, who says in response to her lesbian relationship, 'I would never say no to love. It is so precious that I think that we should open ourselves up to it whenever we find it, no matter what the source.'

Roger

'The garden gets somewhat neglected'

I was first married at the age of twenty-five to a war widow who had a daughter aged two. I was a fairly junior chemist in a big firm where I continued to work for the following four years. I then joined a smaller company and continued my career there and retired at the age of fifty-six, as a result of a stupid decision made by the company when it was taken over. During this period I like to think that we had a normal, happy family relationship. The relationship with my stepdaughter was, and still is, excellent and over the years we have forgotten about the 'step'.

Some two years after my retirement my wife and I moved near the coast, a move partly determined by her love of golf and mine of sailing. We pursued a very active retirement, including doing local voluntary work. Alas, this did not continue, as my wife contracted cancer and after some months of illness she died.

While I was naturally very distressed, I think the fact that I had plenty of warning of what was to be the outcome of her illness helped me to recover fairly quickly. It was no doubt helped by the fact that I deliberately kept myself very active, for example, walking the Dorset coastal path with a friend about two weeks later.

Now, to go back a little more than forty years, before our marriage my wife and I used to spend quite a lot of time with one of my colleagues and one of her school friends, playing tennis and indulging other youthful activities. Some time after we married the other two did likewise. We kept in touch, though living at opposite ends of the country. My colleague died (also from

171

cancer) some twelve years before my wife and his wife came to my wife's funeral. Within six months we were married. To me, we seemed to have a fairly satisfactory relationship, but apparently she did not agree, as within six months she left me without discussion, merely leaving a note saying that we were incompatible. I endeavoured to effect a reconciliation but without success, so after two years I divorced her. I am quite convinced that there was no third party involved, other than possibly her daughter with whom she went to live.

My next two and a half years were not particularly happy. I kept as actively involved in as many activities as possible, holding various offices in a sailing club, doing voluntary work with meals on wheels, joining the University of the Third Age and the local branch of the Probus Club, a social society; and, I must admit, keeping a weather eye open for suitable women friends. I joined a commercial dating agency and as a result met four or five women, only one of whom was anything like compatible with me, but she was soon found to be terminally ill with cancer. Being a GP she fully realized the implications of her diagnosis and, aware of my earlier history, she suggested that we met no more.

During this period I knew, rather remotely, a woman who had joined our sailing club in order to learn to sail. As far as I was aware she was just another married member, although her husband was never seen. However, it seems that during this period she was at the end of an unsatisfactory marriage and on the occasion of a club cruise she asked if she could join my crew.

From this point on I think that we both realized that we had a lot in common. She is a retired archaeologist and, although this is not a subject I know much about, I do try to talk fairly intelligently about it. We enjoyed each other's company so much that she soon became a permanent crew member and shortly after moved in with me. It was not long before we decided to get married. I think I can say that we are both delighted with the idea and have really enjoyed life for the past two and a half years. Inevitably there are occasional disagreements, but in every case these have been resolved within ten minutes with a hug and a cuddle. I suppose I must mention the physical side of marriage: yes, it is still enjoyable at the age of seventy-two (my wife is ten years younger), although it does take about a week for my batteries to recharge.

You might ask how we spend our time. Busily is the answer. My wife runs literature groups for the University of the Third Age and I belong to two specialist groups, science and technology and geology. She occasionally lectures on archaeological subjects. I am secretary of the sailing club and we do our best to keep fit, swimming every week in the winter and rushing round with meals on wheels. During the summer we do quite a lot of sailing. Last year we spent a month on the Normandy coast and we are planning a month in Holland; that is, after a fortnight in the Greek mountains. Our rather large garden does sometimes get quite neglected.

I am sure that we are far from unique in our enjoyment of old age. I am aware of two couples in our age group who have married during the past year, one couple having previously been friends of many years.

Commentary

This account is typical of that given by many people in the Third Age and should be an encouragement to those who have lost their spouses through bereavement and divorce in later life. It is natural for those in their sixties or seventies to feel very despondent when they are left on their own, as Roger was, at what must seem, at the time, to be the end of life. He mentions that after his second wife left him he felt miserable for two and a half years. His experience with dating organizations is not untypical and may be compared with the following account given by Tina who tried to find a husband by such means. I have no way of knowing how successful such agencies are in finding compatible mates; naturally they do not publish figures relating to their failures.

A feature of this account worth mentioning is that Roger delivers meals on wheels, although he is seventy-two years of age. Few people realize the extent to which retired people provide free services to other old people in the community, quite apart from the fact that often the main carers of the elderly in a domestic situation are other old people, that is, their spouses or siblings. Many younger people are under the impression that pensioners are a mere burden on society.

Roger is an excellent example of an elderly man who is very active and whose happiness is greatly enhanced by having a partner. It is also noteworthy that in his seventies he is still sexually active. He and his wife both belong to that excellent organization the University of the Third Age, a countrywide organization that is steadily growing and which provides a focus for like-minded people to get together for a variety of cultural and leisure activities and is entirely run by its members through local groups. He did not meet his wife through this organization, but it is worth mentioning that it serves many single people as a venue for meeting new potential partners. Admittedly, it has a largely a middle-class membership and the term 'University' puts off some people, who think erroneously that it is devoted entirely to academic pursuits. In fact almost any activity from swimming to coach tours is included in the repertoire of events that the members organize for themselves. Like most people who have contributed to this book Roger is middle class, for, despite my efforts to recruit accounts from as wide a cross-section of society as practicable, inevitably it has been middle-class people who have mainly responded.

Tina
'I still love him dearly'

The first time I talked to Angus at length was at a house-warming luncheon at a new neighbour's. Everyone living near by was invited and he, widowed a few months before and newly returned from a holiday with friends, had to be persuaded by his hosts to come. I suppose I was attracted to him immediately, although when I had met him casually before in the company of his wife Joan I had just regarded him as a nice enough man who was her partner. I'm sure that it was just sympathy for his loneliness and grief that prompted me on our walk back towards our houses to say, 'I well remember what it was like when I was first alone and how much I missed someone to talk to. If you ever feel in need of a chat, do ring and come and have a drink or a meal.'

On the Wednesday he phoned and on the Thursday he came to dinner. I dressed myself up in a pretty long cotton skirt and lit candles on the dinner table. He arrived with flowers for me.

Conversation was easy. I drew him into talking about his business, and he was surprised and pleased that I could understand his problems. He had told me at the party that he was working all hours to redress the decline the company had gone into while he was nursing his dying wife the year before. My ex-husband had worked in industry and we had moved to Scotland, where he started up in a business partnership with a friend. Alas, it hadn't worked out, and my marriage break-up was one of the results of the fiasco. I had listened to a lot of shop talk in the thirty-odd years we were together.

We moved away from the table to drink our coffee, sitting across the room from one another. Suddenly Angus stretched out and said, 'Why are you sitting over there? Why don't you come sit beside me on the couch?' In no time at all I was in his arms and we were kissing hungrily, blissfully. The body chemistry was working and soon we were in my bed making wonderful, passionate love. Alas, the enforced celibacy during the long months of Joan's illness affected his sexual performance and quite unnecessarily he was upset. Falling asleep in his arms was a joy I had not expected to experience again.

The next morning I smuggled him out early, not wanting neighbours to know what was going on. Before he went he said something that has remained in my memory ever since: 'It was all wonderful. I didn't think I could enjoy love-making ever again, but I don't know how permanent this can be.' I replied, 'Who's talking about things being permanent? Let's just enjoy today!' Our relationship was to remain 'permanent' for seven years.

We saw more and more of each other, enjoying one another's company. To begin with most of his conversation centred on his wife, whom he had loved deeply throughout their marriage, and his business. This I encouraged because I saw it as a way of helping him come to terms with his bereavement. The difference in our backgrounds and upbringing was noticeable. He was the eldest child of a large, working-class country family, denied his place at a grammar school through lack of money and apprenticed in a factory a few days after his fourteenth birthday. I was an only child in a middle-class family with a private education and no responsibilities. We differed in our religious beliefs, our political party allegiances, our choice of homes and furnishings and, most of all, in leisure pursuits. He was a sports and fitness fanatic, watching everything and anything sporty on television. He was obsessed with angling (describing his addiction to it as a disease) and as a younger man was very involved in road cycling. In middle age he took it up again as exercise and regularly cycled forty miles or so.

Yet, as our relationship deepened into a loving friendship, we found that we had quite a lot in common, not least being that we were both sensual people, expressing our affection with a passing kiss, a touch to the face, a ruffling of the hair, a squeeze of the hand and, at nights, in our now near-perfect love-making. We were delighted but surprised to discover that a grandmother in her late fifties and a grandfather in his sixties could enjoy these wonderful intimacies; both of us slim, and he only a little taller than me, our bodies fitted together perfectly. I was always turned on by his neat little bottom and firm, lean thighs and he said that my smooth skin and tiny breasts excited him at a touch. Did others of our acquaintance feel the same way? we wondered, and doubted it. It appeared that most of our friends, now notching up around forty years of marriage, had lost interest in one another, and we congratulated ourselves on finding love a second time.

I don't think that I made a conscious decision to love Angus. Our closeness and our living together, as we almost were, presupposed this. I wasn't madly in love with him as I had been with my husband in my youth, seeing in him the perfect man of my dreams. I loved Angus for his warmth, his loving care of me, his generosity and, above all, his kindness and good humour, but I recognized his faults and would have changed them gladly if I could. He, too, was well aware of mine; the worst were my occasional short, sharp bursts of temper, quickly over and forgotten, and a tendency to complain about things I don't like rather than putting up with them. I often turned to him and said 'I love you' when he had done or said something that stirred me, but hardly ever did he reciprocate, and I concluded that he found it difficult to actually express his love in words.

The question of marriage was talked about on one or two occasions in a vague way and always Angus concluded that it would not be a good idea. He was afraid that if we were together all day, every day, our relationship might break down. In many ways I longed to be his wife. Although liaisons such as ours are now accepted, friends were always asking me when we were going to get married and on our holidays together I found it very embarrassing that people assumed that we were a married couple. In my heart that is what I wanted us to be.

Looking back, I realize I never told him that I wanted to be married, for several reasons: to begin with, I'm old-fashioned enough to believe that a woman should wait until a man proposes; secondly, the question of whose home we would live in was going to be a tricky one to resolve. Angus said many times that he wouldn't want to leave his house – and Joan's house – including the garden Joan had created and her ashes which he had scattered there. I, meanwhile, much preferred my rooms with their traditional period furnishings, where there was enough room for my family to stay. We could have compromised on this, I am sure, if we had really wanted to get married, but I, too, was nervous of committing myself again. I'd been through some very unhappy times in my marriage as well as a very traumatic divorce, and I couldn't bear the thought of going through all that a second time.

Our arrangement suited his needs extremely well. He was free to enjoy his leisure pursuits, to go away on fishing trips and to take his only grandson (whose father, Angus's and Joan's only son, had been killed in an accident a year before Joan's death) away on holiday each year. After the first Christmas trip abroad he went every year, at first for two weeks, then four, finally six. He took his fishing tackle with him, together with the Christmas gifts for his friends – which I had suggested, bought, wrapped and packed – and spent most of his time on his own deep-sea fishing. I hated his being away and missed him dreadfully. Angus was not a letter-writer, and I looked forward to his occasional phone calls, always one on Christmas morning and New Year's Eve, saying he missed me. We both knew that there was no possibility of my accompanying him, as I had a job and had family commitments, mainly with regard to my father. Each year Angus would say, 'Perhaps next year you'll be able to come.'

His business was prospering. Angus was making money and was always happy to share it with me. We had a much more expensive lifestyle than I was used to, eating and drinking well at home and at restaurants. He bought me expensive birthday and Christmas presents and gifts from his holidays. Every year he took me on a sunshine holiday, both of us being sun and sea worshippers. Angus would hire a car and we spent idyllic days in solitary coves and happy family evenings at the best restaurants in town.

It was a great bonus that Angus got on so well with my children and they, of course, could hardly fail to like him. My younger daughter was just sixteen when my husband left us for another woman. Angus became his replacement and she, in turn, was the daughter he had always longed for.

My life was very full but happier than I had ever thought it would be again after my marriage breakdown. I had an interesting secretarial job in the mornings (getting that had been the turning point on my road to recovery from the divorce trauma). I was appreciative of all that Angus did for me and often, when thanking him, chided him for spoiling me so much. His answer was almost always the same: 'Oh, love, it's a two-way thing. Just think what you have done and still do for me.' That, I thought, is true love: each of us giving to the other and not realizing that we were doing so.

In 1988 Angus was unable to spend Christmas abroad with his friends, as they were planning a family visit elsewhere. Unknown to me, my younger daughter persuaded him that he should take advantage of the bargain airfares on offer and take me abroad in the autumn to visit my elder daughter. With the New Year came the bad weather and Angus's daily outdoor activities of cycling and fishing were severely curtailed. He had officially retired on New Year's Day and now went to his office only irregularly. He took to visiting a health club in the nearby town. Every afternoon he would go for a work-out and often in the evening over dinner he would tell me how unfit he was compared with some of the 'girls' who were there. He hated the bad weather and was missing the sunshine, the beaches and the fishing he enjoyed abroad.

It was around this time that one spring evening, after we had had a few cross words (which seldom happened), he asked me if I would like our relationship to end. I was amazed by his suggestion and certainly didn't take it seriously, but at the same time I assured him that nothing was further from my mind. I couldn't imagine life without him. So secure was I in my love for him, and what I believed was his for me, that no warning bells rang.

The next few weeks were not happy ones. Somehow things didn't seem to be quite right between Angus and me, but I put it down to my being overwrought. One evening when my daughter was having dinner with us, he casually mentioned to her that he was going away on a fishing trip the following week for a few days. This was the first I had heard of it and I was upset that he had not mentioned it to me. A few weeks earlier I had told him that I was attending the Women's Institute annual general meeting at the beginning of June at the Albert Hall and thought it would be an opportunity to visit my sister-in-law near London for a couple of nights. He said he would look after my dog to save putting him in kennels.

The night before Angus left for his trip he decided that we should sleep in our own houses as he was making an early start. When I left him after dinner, I wished him a happy trip and then thoughtlessly added, 'I'm sure your few days away will do you good. I only wish you hadn't been so sneaky about it.' On my way back I realized I shouldn't have said that, and as soon as I got home I phoned him to apologize. He was a bit short but accepted my apology and I thought we parted amicably.

I received no phone call from him and, as I didn't know the name of his hotel, I could not phone him. After a week I called into his office to ask his manager and secretary if he had been in touch with them or whether they had his hotel telephone number. 'You know how casual Angus is,' they said. 'We never know where he is.' Somehow I had the feeling they knew but wouldn't tell me. The following week, with still no word, worried and upset I left for the meeting in London, after putting the dog into kennels.

I returned three days later. There was no reply from Angus's phone. Was he still away on his trip or had he simply gone out fishing for the day? I unpacked and fetched the dog, then Angus answered the phone next time I called. Our conversation was strained, but he invited me to supper as usual. It will be all right again, I thought; once we're together we'll overcome whatever has come between us; probably in bed tonight.

I was greeted by Angus with a kiss and a drink as usual, and he cooked his speciality: steak. As we ate, he told me in great detail about the breakdown of his sports BMW, which had kept him away for two weeks, how the agents in the nearest town had failed to repair it and how he had had to wait for a spare part to be sent. I listened sympathetically. His car was his pride and joy. His tale told, I was now free to ask the burning question: 'But why didn't you phone and let me know what was happening?' 'I didn't want to phone,' came the reply. 'I wanted to tell you face to face.' My heart leapt into my mouth. 'I wanted to tell you that as far as I am concerned our relationship is over. I can't put up with your complaining and your outbursts of temper any more.'

He reminded me of all the occasions when I had lost my temper; they were forgotten by me, but he had remembered every one in detail. I was in shock. I heard what he said but couldn't reply. He had met another woman to whom he was very attracted, one of the 'girls' from the health club. They had more in common than he and I: she was keen on sports and exercise; she rode a bike and enjoyed fishing. She had been away with him on the holiday and he had been teaching her to fish for salmon. He continued explaining why he could no longer live with me. Only half-attending, I remembered him saying how good I'd been for him, how I'd helped him through his bad times, how much I had done for him and how that last ill-chosen remark had finally killed any love he had had for me. He had interpreted it as resentment on my part of his going away without me. I wanted to cry, 'Can't you see it was hurt that you didn't share your plans with me? As a couple I thought we shared everything.'

I don't believe I uttered a word. We still sat at the table over the remains of dinner and I watched a glorious sunset through the picture window. My mind was reeling, my thoughts whirling. This isn't happening; it's a bad dream. I'll wake up and Angus will take me in his arms and comfort me as he always does when I have a bad dream. Not this time; he doesn't love you any more. He's got another woman. She must be young and lissome and wonderfully healthy. He's always attracted by lovely bodies and fitness. This is why he's been going to the club every day. Why didn't I suspect? Because he has told me many times that he's a one-woman man, that he had never been unfaithful to his wife. I have always known him as a truthful, honourable man. I've been so sure of his love for me. Perhaps it will be just an affair. He'll come back to me. He's not a philanderer like John, my ex-husband. This man takes a long time to make a decision but, once made, he won't change his mind. He means it. If only we had been married this wouldn't have happened. I'm sure he wouldn't have been unfaithful then.

It was quite dark and we sat in silence. Suddenly Angus switched on the light and began to clear the table. I got up. 'I'd better go home,' I said and went into the bedroom. Without realizing what I was doing, I collected up my spare dressing-gown and slippers and my makeup and toilet things that had lived there for a long time. I walked out of the house without a word and out of Angus's life.

Afterwards I had a mental picture of him watching to see the lights go on in my house across the gardens, picking up the phone and saying to her, 'I've told her. She's gone and I'm free.'

The next days, weeks and months were a living hell, just as they are for anybody who has been suddenly bereaved. The disbelief, the aloneness, the fear of the future, together with the inability to eat and sleep, and the uncontrollable bouts of crying – and in my case a strong desire for alcohol to shut out the pain – were all part of my grief. I had been through this before, fourteen years earlier, and I had been equally bereft then. But my husband had gone off to live in another country. Angus was living on my doorstep, and I could hear the distinctive sound of his car coming and going, and it seemed like sod's law that we would encounter one another by chance in the drive.

The weather was very hot and, as I walked my dog in the cool of the evening, I would meet him on his way out, beautifully dressed as always in his expensive casual clothes, and I knew where he was going. Sometimes I would hear him return in the early morning. If we met by chance we were like strangers, making polite conversation and, as we talked, the longing for him, to touch his dear face, to hold his hand, was unbearable. I would continue my walk down the fields or return home and weep uncontrollably.

One morning I saw him returning from his bike ride. I went to his house and found him lying on his secluded lawn, without any clothes on, recovering from his exertions. I calmly asked him to reconsider his decision. I found out that the lissome young gold-digger I had imagined was, in fact, a widow, only a few years younger than myself, who worked at the gym because she was in a dancing troupe. This, I realized sadly, was a different matter. He told me he intended to get to know her better as he felt he wanted to spend the rest of his life with her and, if it didn't work out, he would be very lonely. My loneliness didn't come into it: 'There had never been any commitment between us,' he said. After seven years of happiness with him, it was a lifetime's commitment on my part, whether we were married or not.

All pride forgotten, I broke down. I begged him to give me another chance to re-establish the happiness we had had. Why was he punishing me so cruelly for faults that he had always known I possessed? He was immovable. As I left him he said, 'You've been very good for me during the past years. You're still a very attractive woman with a lot to offer, and you'll soon find someone else to take my place. We can still be friends.'

He knows my character as well as I do and has often remarked that I see everything as black or white and can't accept the grey. He knows only too well that after the years of intimacy we had shared I could never accept being just friends. And as far as meeting someone else, he knew I had met no one in the seven years I was on my own before he came along and in the age group I was now in was even less likely to

During the next month or two I deteriorated mentally and physically. Depression set in. I became suicidal at one point and planned my death. However, my plans were thwarted and I never quite had the courage to try again. My father had died and I spent day after day on my own in his old home cleaning it out, desperately trying to make rational decisions. The bric-à-brac accumulated over sixty years of a happy marriage saddened me greatly.

Angus moved in with his new lady love in the nearby town. He came over each day to collect mail and check on his house, and we accidentally met from time to time in the drive. If she was with him he passed by, but alone he would stop and ask how I was. Couldn't he see? Thin, my face was drawn with hollow eyes, a face I found hard to recognize as mine at times when it faced me in the bathroom mirror. These meetings filled me with pain. My heart pounded, my legs turned to jelly, I was consumed with a desire to touch him. I was longing to know what he was doing, how he filled his life, but often the answers to my questions hurt deeply. 'They' were going to Cornwall for August; 'they' were going to London to stay (as I had done many times) with his friends who were over here on one of their frequent trips; and, most hurtful of all, 'they' were going abroad for Christmas. And this was the Christmas that I was at last free to go.

I could not come to terms with the fact that I was no longer part of his life. The next time he stopped to talk I told him to drive on in future. I didn't want to talk to him any more; it was too hurtful. We now pass as if we were strangers.

Living in a small community, everybody knows everything, and it wasn't long before the neighbours were aware of what had happened. The closest ones, with whom we had had a good social life, were very sympathetic and jollied me along with remarks such as 'You mustn't be on your own too much; you must go out', 'Come and see us whenever you need company' and 'You'll soon find somebody else.' I accepted gratefully their invitations, but as our community consists almost entirely of couples, I was very conscious of being on my own, and conversation was often a strain, all references to Angus being carefully avoided.

Unlike a bereavement through death, no public sympathy could be expressed. No prayers could be said in church for the grieving Mrs So-and-so, nor could I expect an official visit from our rector. When I was in the depths of depression, attendance at our tiny church, with its congregation of no more than fifteen, was little consolation. As a regular worshipper my absence would have been noticeable, yet I found no comfort in the services. 'Love thy neighbour as thyself,' said the Commandments – and hadn't I done that and thanked God each week for bringing 'my neighbour' into my life? My faith has never been very strong. I have always had doubts and I think I probably attend church more as a moral discipline than as a believer. After listening to an interesting sermon on the power of prayer, I asked our curate, whom I knew had trained in counselling, to visit me. For several weeks I got comfort from his visits. I was able to unburden myself, and he gave me helpful books to read. I doubted that such a young man could understand the depth of my unhappiness: the longing for the person you love, who has deliberately chosen to remove himself from you because you were found wanting. Humiliation, lack of self-confidence, bitterness and jealousy are not the usual accompaniments to grief resulting from death, I thought.

I decided that the only way I would get over Angus was to fill his place in my life and I made inquiries about marriage bureaux. I joined one in the next county. The proprietor, herself divorced and remarried, was kind, sympathetic and over-confident, as I later discovered. I had lunch with several men in the first few weeks. The lack of mutual attraction was obvious. Because the ratio of women to men in the sixties to seventies age group is so vast, I knew from a friend who had also joined the bureau that we were being shared out among the few men available. Over the months the number of available males dwindled, although the proprietor used all her resources to remedy this. New membership to women over sixty was soon closed. I have resisted renewing my subscription. Six or seven introductions (and only one of these that I would have wanted to know better) was a poor return for a lot of money. Driving sixty miles to meet a widowed farmer who was obviously looking for a replacement farmer's wife brought home yet again how incredibly lucky I was to have met Angus. Not for the first time did I curse my stupidity in allowing my volatile temperament to destroy the wonderful relationship that had developed between us.

As time has passed, Angus and his lady friend have spent more time at his house. At first it was for weekends, but now they come for weeks on end, and the sound – so distinctive and so well loved – of his car, the noise of his motor-mower, the sight of them working together in the garden and the lights showing through the trees in the evenings fill me with anguish. I hear my neighbours talking to one another as they go to bed and get up in the mornings, and I feel very alone.

My thoughts are constantly with him, remembering our lifestyle and habits and wondering whether it is still the same for Angus and 'her'. I wonder whether she is a better cook than me and whether she makes him his favourite dishes. Does he express his approval of her choice of clothes as he always did of mine? Does he talk about his wife – and me? Does she feel my presence there in the home, in the same way that I was always conscious of Joan's? And, of course, the question that hurts most, 'Is their love-making even better than he said ours was?' I knew from the beginning of the break-up, and told Angus so, that there would be no room in this small community for the three of us. I knew that I would never be able to accept their presence together here but that others would. They already have, and I find it very hurtful that mere neighbours know what is going on in his life while I, who for so long knew his every thought, know nothing.

For two years I harboured the fantasy that Angus's new relationship would founder, that he would experience my despair and loneliness and, in time, he would come back to me and we would be together for all the time we have left. More recently I have fantasized that I would at last meet another man, loving and lovable, who would wipe away all the hurt, the jealousy, the bitterness and, above all, the self-hate that I have experienced and restore me to being the warm, caring and loving person that I really am. However, common sense now prevails. I know Angus is to be married soon and they plan to sell both their homes and make a fresh start. Eventually he will be out of my sight, I hope for ever. And I now know that I must face up to the fact that, like millions of other women in their sixties, life has to be lived, in a way that we don't want or well enjoy, but to the best of our ability. My immediate concern now must be for my daughter who, at thirty-five, has chosen to become a single mother. Once again I must become a 'carer' and hope that the joys and worries that this new life will bring will, in time, ease my longing for the man I still love so dearly.

Commentary

'We can still be friends' is what Tina's lover said to her when he made it clear that he wished to end their relationship. She regarded this as an impossible suggestion. I do not think it is particularly significant that Tina was in her fifties and her lover in his sixties, for it is an example of what can happen to anyone at any stage in their lives: being abandoned by a trusted lover. Early on in the narrative the reader may have anticipated the sad end of the relationship: after all, the couple did not have much in common; it was their sensuality that created the greatest bond between them, and I think Tina was a little blind to her lover's detachment. He would not respond when she told him she loved him and, as their mutual acquaintances told her, he was a loner – fishing and solo cycling were his hobbies.

It appears to have been quite early on that he asked her, after an argument, if she would like their relationship to end. He knew that she had been abandoned by her husband, and this may have been said as a threat. I have the impression that all along he regarded the relationship as somewhat temporary.

I found this account moving and respect Tina for her frankness, including her description of her breakdown when she begged Angus to take her back. It reminded me of the letter written by Marian (George Eliot) to Herbert Spencer described in Chapter 5.

Tina is clearly a woman who has a great deal of love to give and who is truly fulfilled only in a loving relationship with a man. Her account illustrates very poignantly the unenviable position of so many women in later life who are the victims of the growing numerical discrepancy between men and women in later life. Her account of her efforts to find a husband through a dating agency and of learning that some of them have closed their books to women over the age of sixty is certainly a sign of the times. The old taboos are crumbling, and it is now quite respectable for older women to want a man; but with this freedom comes the frustration that such a need cannot be met for a great many women. They find themselves in the humiliating position of being a commodity in a buyers' market.

This story does not end on an entirely sad note, for Tina finds solace in the traditional role of grandmother: her grandchild will benefit from Tina's evident need to give love.

Tom
'The man with two front doors'

I am the man with two front doors and two homes. In 1976 my wife and I left our urban house to live in the country, taking over two adjacent cottages. We modernized and added extensions to these old buildings but retained the two front doors. Owing to my failing health, several years later we moved to a small house in a neighbouring town. After a few quite happy years there, my wife died and I went on living in the empty house.

I need not describe the years of desolation and depression that followed my bereavement, for that is not at all unusual, and I believe that many older men die during the first year following the death of their wives. I certainly felt at the time that this would be a satisfactory culmination to my life. I had my work and spent many hours in the reading room of a library where I saw other old men, like myself, some of them becoming rather like dried-up tortoises, with their slow movements and scholar's stoop. This is how I expected to end up, but two circumstances set me on another path. First, I became acquainted with the later writings of Alex Comfort and, second, I met Helen.

Comfort's writings opened my eyes to the fact that the term 'old' is relative. Because one has had a certain number of birthdays one does not necessarily become a special sort of person, an 'old man,' destined to fulfil a prescribed role and, in my case, to become a scholarly tortoise. I became aware of the huge mythology about ageing with which I had grown up; some of this I had unthinkingly accepted. Now, I realized, much of it was simply untrue. Looking at myself, I saw that all sorts of changes had taken place to my physical being – the falling out of teeth, the greying of hair, the lessening of muscular stamina – but essentially, in my seventies, I was the same person as I had always been. When people treated me as an 'old man' I felt that I was a bit of a fraud, posing behind a mask like a Greek actor. I did not want to dress in trendy clothes or to adopt the outward trappings of any particular age, for that would be posing too. I just wanted to be . . . myself. For the first time I realized how contemporary society attempts to curb and delineate the role of the older section of the population. We had witnessed a minor revolution in attitudes with regard to the negative aspects of racism and sexism, but few people seemed aware of the strength and influence of ageist prejudice.

One of the things about me that at first awakened Helen's interest was that I had two front doors to my old house in the country. I don't know why this amused and intrigued her, but this peculiarity of my house contributed to her decision to get know me better. She did not know how prophetic of our future relationship this was, for I was once again to have two front doors – mine and hers – and to sleep at both houses. So why do we not have just one front door and sleep together in one house like any other sensible couple? That involves a consideration of some of the peculiarities of love in later life and the different experiences Helen and I have had in our earlier marriages.

After some months of being good friends, our friendship became affectionate to the degree of holding hands on the sofa. One thing I was quite clear about: it would be useless to expect Helen to come to bed with me in the immediate future. I remember thinking: Give it perhaps another year. Holding hands and shy kisses were very delightful. I thought that I knew women for, after all, I had lived in the world for over seventy years and my associates had been a very bohemian crowd who had anticipated the 'swinging sixties' in the 'thrusting thirties'. Helen was very shy and did not like to meet my eye when we were alone together. She had experienced a marriage that ended in divorce very unhappily and had every reason to distrust men. I counted it a great victory on my part that, after months of friendship and writing each other letters, I had at last got her to sit beside me on the settee and hold my hand!

I decided that the best thing to do was to try to express myself in a letter, telling her of my deep appreciation of what our friendship meant to me and how I understood her reluctance to come closer to me in a physical sense. I assured her that this reluctance would make absolutely no difference to the closeness of our affectionate friendship. But I begged her not to rule out completely the possibility that one day we might be lovers in a physical sense. It was a long letter and utterly sincere, for I really did envisage a possible future in which we remained the best of friends, contributing to one another's happiness but never actually making love. After all, I was in my seventies and she was in her sixties, and I didn't know much about love in later life. I felt much the same, but did she?

I took several days composing the letter, but I never really finished it. I did not need to, for Aphrodite, who had been watching us with amusement from Olympus for some time, took pity on us and suddenly threw her mantle over us. What an ass I had been! How blind I had been to all the signs on Helen's part that had amused the goddess so much. In Helen's bed I learned just how passionate a woman in her sixties can be.

After we had been lovers for about two months, I proposed marriage to her, couching my proposal in a letter which I put in her hand as I left her bedside one night to sleep elsewhere. In my letter I tried to list all the reasons why she might not wish to marry me, but I hoped that the positive aspects of our sharing a home would outweigh the negative ones. I was quite certain that she was the only woman for me and that we could make each other happy. And indeed I still think this after four years of our relationship, I am sure of it. But she refused my proposal. She still wanted to go on living on her own, which is why there continue to be two front doors. As time went on, she told me the reasons why she did not want to marry me and, interestingly, they were not quite the reasons that I had listed in my letter of proposal. There were some I hadn't thought of.

The trite maxim that 'One is never too old to learn' certainly applies in one's seventies and I will probably learn a great deal more in my eighties. My relationship with Helen has certainly opened up a whole new field of knowledge to me. I had no idea that life at this period of the natural span could be so exciting, so rewarding. Sometimes when we are embarking on some new venture she says to me, 'The adventure continues!' and so it does. I have learned also some of the complications of growing old in our society and, in particular, the difficulties of being a woman, for the roles ageing women are expected to fulfil are rather more prescribed than those of men.

Early on in our partnership as lovers I discovered how she was involved in a difficult conflict of roles in relation to her children and grandchildren. After leaving her impossible husband, from whom she obtained a divorce, she lived on her own for about eight years and settled down fairly peacefully as a single woman. She greatly valued her new-found independence after over thirty years of being a wife and mother and looked forward to a placid future. But of course to her family she was 'Grandma', a figure who has a defined role in society, especially when she is, through bereavement or divorce, living on her own. 'Grandma' acts as a stand-in for 'Mother' when required: she is a figure of benevolent authority and the custodian of traditional moral values. One expects her to be a bit old-fashioned in her ways and to provide a stable background. Such a role is not expected of 'Grandpa', for he, after all, is a man.

In this particular family Grandpa had remarried and even taken his new wife with him to visit the house of his eldest daughter, where there were little girls approaching their teens. It may have been a little shocking for the girls to have their grandfather taking a woman to bed with him who was a stranger to the family. I do not really know how the children reacted to this situation. Were they old enough to appreciate the implications of it? But when I came on the scene and was taken to stay at their house, the problem arose of my status. I was not married to Grandma. Did I go to bed with her? Well, no, for one of the little girls turned out of her bedroom and I slept among her less-favoured soft toys. But as I tiptoed back across the landing from Helen's room late at night, I heard delighted giggles coming from the little girls' room. 'What was Grandma up to?' they were obviously wondering.

Thus poor Helen was in a state of role conflict there and could not act quite naturally with anyone when I was around. I found myself treated by her with surprising coldness and, it seemed to me, unnecessary rudeness in front of the family. She was, of course, trying to make the point that she was still Grandma, the custodian of traditional values and not a floozy in her sixties who had kicked over the traces. She did her best in a difficult situation and I appreciate that one cannot be entirely rational or natural when in a state of conflict over one's roles.

She could, of course, have married me and thus given me equal status with her ex-husband's new wife in the eyes of the family, but although this would have resolved one role conflict it would have generated others. When she left her husband – with every reason in the world for doing so – she made an oath to herself that she would never fall into the marriage trap again. She had played a demanding role for over thirty years with loyalty and devotion, and what did she get at the end of it? A situation that was an utter betrayal of all she had a right to expect.

In her fairly placid single life, she had never dreamed that she might get a lover ever again. The whole idea seemed bizarre to her. And then, quite out of the blue, a lover had materialized, persistently wooed her and eventually won her. In doing so he had awakened in her a passionate nature she never knew she possessed. How could this new role – the role of an excited 'bride' – be squared with that of being a respectable grandmother?

Things were much better in the homes of her other married children, for there the grandchildren were only little tots, who came into our bed in the morning and played like puppies, quite taking the situation for granted. As Mummy had a man – their father – in her bed to cuddle her, so Grandma had her bed-companion – me. In the few years I have known them, the children have taken me for granted and they even sometimes bring us breakfast in bed. I have been fortunate in that Helen's children are not only very fond of her but are sensible enough to realize that I have contributed to her happiness and so I am a welcome figure. I have heard one of her daughters inviting a friend to 'come and meet Ma's toyboy'.

A woman in Helen's position has even further conflicts to contend with. During her years of being alone she had grown friendly with a number of women who were also living singly after divorce. There is, of course, a great shortage of men in the older decades of life. These women felt great solidarity among themselves and counted on one another for practical and emotional support. The fact that Helen had taken a lover could be seen as a kind of betrayal of her close women friends and could even conceivably arouse envy. As we continued to live in separate houses, she would sometimes leave a friend's house at night ostensibly to return to her own house but really to come to my bed.

This element of furtiveness in our relationship had its funny side. We lived in adjacent roads and were supplied by the same milkman who collected the week's money on Friday mornings. If Helen was spending the night at my house, I would often throw on a dressing-gown and go down to pay him, then add that I wanted to pay Mrs T's bill as well. 'She's out, is she?' he would ask with a knowing grin, perfectly well aware that she was upstairs in my bedroom. In the same way, Helen would sometimes pay my bill as well as her own if I was sleeping at her house. The milkman knew perfectly well what our relationship was and treated her with heavy gallantry. I was reminded of the well-known song by Fats Waller, 'My Very Good Friend the Milkman Said . . .' Here the milkman frankly advised marriage, but our milkman gets more fun out of our not being married or living together.

I have written up till now as though all our difficulties stemmed from her conflict of roles, but that is by no means the case. There are difficulties in my family which I prefer not to write about and, because of them, living with me would not be entirely easy. Helen therefore feels more secure behind her own front door, where she can retreat and be mistress of her own territory. I have a key to that door, just as she has a key to mine. Sometimes she makes me feel that her house is my second home and she refers to the bed in the front room as 'your' bed. It is almost as though it were 'our' house, and I am happy to do small chores such as cleaning the lavatory from time to time. On some occasions, however, I am made to feel that I am simply a guest and the formal constraints on a guest must be observed. Sometimes when I go there she greets me rather formally and it takes a little while for the ice to break between us; at other times she greet me delightedly, warmly, putting her arms round me and telling me how glad she is to see me. As for my house, she insists on cleaning the kitchen, even dusting the sitting-room occasionally, against all my protests and, really, against her declared principles. For when I first knew her she impressed on me that she never intended to do housewifely duties for anyone ever again. Of course I know that she loves me dearly, as I love her.

In the first year of our association as lovers I was sometimes deeply miserable over these two front doors, an unhappiness I generally tried to conceal from her. I wanted us to live together like any other loving couple, but with her past traumatic experience of an unhappy marriage break-up she did not want us to be a 'couple'. She even said that it might be better if I found myself a 'wife'. But I do not want a wife. I want her. I am perfectly capable of managing my own domestic affairs. I proposed marriage to her: I wanted to 'love, honour and cherish, till death do us part', and this is still my desire. She is utterly unique in my life – a woman in her sixties with a wrinkled face who is the joy of my desiring and my saviour from what I might have become. Like me she has a puritan background but with a pagan joy of life.

So I settled for half a loaf and two front doors. In my blacker moods I would comfort myself with the thought that as I was 'old', the conflict would be resolved relatively soon by the angel of death. Perhaps that was in her mind too.

If one loves in old age, one must accept that one's feelings may be as stormy as they were in one's youth. For me, and I suspect for many, age makes no difference at all to one's love life. My love for Helen has been one of the greatest and most rewarding of my experiences in a not unadventurous life. Not only do we have a great deal of joy and sheer fun when we are together, but she has inspired me to be a much more creative person in my work. I have been glad to write this testimony to the power that loving has to keep us human and living vitally, and I hope it will encourage others to realize that, although our bodies may wrinkle and wither, our spirits can stay as fresh and adventurous as ever.

Commentary

Tom's experience must be typical of many men in later life who have been rendered single by bereavement or divorce. Being of a generation that had a definite view of what old age would be like, on the death of his wife he expected to conform to that stereotype and to become old, lonely and withered. He mentions the writings of Alex Comfort, which opened his eyes to a different view of later life that served to put him on the road to striving for a new kind of lifestyle. Undoubtedly Comfort, along with other popular writers who are quite revolutionary in their views of ageing, has had a powerfully liberating effect on the mores of older people.

Tom mentions fellow scholars who are 'rather like dried-up tortoises' and he had expected to become like them but, even if he had not read Comfort or had the good fortune to meet Helen, the chances of a man such as he becoming one of the liberated members of the Third Age are quite good, for there are many factors in the modern world that are highly favourable. Not least of these is the great preponderance of women over men in the older decades, which gives a man a wide choice among suitable partners if he is at all minded to form a new relationship.

It is interesting to note that Tom, conforming to the expectations of the age in which he grew up, appeared to assume that a respectable middle-class woman such as Helen would want to marry him once they had formed a sexual relationship. In fact she upset his assumptions that an older woman would wish to be respectably married, preferring to live as his 'mistress', thereby flouting age-old conventions. Undoubtedly she felt some hesitancy over this, for she displayed some embarrassment over her position and had him sleep in a separate bedroom at the house where her older grandchildren lived. Where the grandchildren were much younger she did not bother, for they might be expected to grow up in the sexually liberated climate of the modern age.

The acceptance of two people continuing to have separate homes while virtually living together, as in the case of Tom and his lover, obviously reflects a certain degree of middle-class affluence, for maintaining two houses in these circumstances would be beyond the economic means of those on lower incomes.

Vera

'My love is not returned,
but I am content'

I am a widow of seventy-six. I lost my husband two years ago. At first I was devastated and, in spite of the wonderful support from my family, I could not really contemplate continuing my life. In due course I was encouraged by an old and distant friend to find myself a voluntary job and make a new life for myself. I am now very much in love with the friend concerned. At my great age I did not recognize what was happening at first, but am now delighted to be so alive and happy. The world is a warm and welcoming world and so newly beautiful. My love is not returned, but I have this very lovely friendship and I am content with the warmth and support that I receive. I would never have thought it possible to feel so happy and vital at my age.

Commentary

In collecting autobiographical accounts of people's experiences of love in later life I received this brief account and thought little of it, but the author came to see me after visiting her friend and told me a great deal about her relationship. I can only describe her as being 'all aglow' with love in a manner not usually apparent in older people. She had had a long and quite happy, if not exciting, marriage to a man in a minor profession and this 'old and distant friend' had not meant much to her during those years of marriage. She seemed anxious to confide to me, a complete stranger, quite a lot about herself, including the fact that she was now truly in love and experiencing feelings reminiscent of those she had had as an adolescent before meeting her husband.

She intimated rather shyly that she had once been in love when she was very young and that it had meant a great deal to her. She had not discussed this experience with her husband and they had had a very peaceful and uneventful marriage. She admitted that it took her some time to come to terms with her bereavement, but almost guiltily she then found that there were compensations in being a single woman instead of a wife very much devoted to her husband's needs.

Her falling in love with the old family friend had been a very moving experience and she was quite surprised at herself. She had not let her friend know of her new feelings for him and I got the impression that he would have been very embarrassed if he had known. It might be thought that not being able to tell him, or to consummate her love in any way would have been very frustrating and a cause for sadness but, on the contrary, it somehow enhanced her appreciation of life and she was able to write, 'The world is a warm and welcoming world and so newly beautiful.'

This was no passing event for Vera. It was four years ago that I talked with her and recently I had a letter from her. Now in her eighties she lives in an old people's home and her happiness is still enhanced by this love for a man she seldom sees. She writes, 'Alas, the love is still one-sided. I have accepted this quite happily.' For her there appears to be an almost mystical component of this love, and I wonder how common this kind of love is in later life.

Charlie

'Few would guess Bill will be eighty this summer'

The magical factor in my life today after a quarter of a century as a widower is William, or Bill, as he insists on being called. Bill will be eighty this summer, but few could guess his secret. Tall, erect, with a wonderful head of silver hair, elegantly dressed, Bill carries himself like a guardsman in a hurry. By nature he is a cross between a human dynamo and a pressure cooker; usually around six o'clock he runs out of steam. Then I can begin to care for him.

Bill moved into my maisonette last autumn, but it is six years since we first met. A mutual friend asked him to pick me up and bring me to his birthday party. He drove very fast for a man of his age and when he reached the house he whipped a case of wine from the boot of his car and skipped down the dozen steps to the basement entrance. I was impressed. Later I discovered that his ability to run up and down steps like a ten-year-old is something he is always eager to show off. As the evening progressed I thought him a pompous ass. He talked at people; didn't listen. It was much later that I understood that in his fifteen years without a partner his strategy of learning new skills – cooking, laundering, cleaning and photography – had not lessened his loneliness. He needed to talk, and a party was a golden opportunity.

We became close friends. We each owned a flat, seven miles apart, and we both ran a car, so for six years we commuted to and from one another's home. Like most men of his generation Bill has worked very hard – as a surveyor – with seldom more than two weeks' annual holiday. So each year he had returned to Devon and Cornwall. I was astonished that he had never ventured further. But he has taken to travel like the proverbial duck to water. Together we have spent time in Majorca, Malta, Estoril, Tenerife, the Costa del Sol and Paris. He has now a row of photograph albums as a record and his conversation is richer for our delightful adventures.

A year ago I had eight toes broken surgically and reset. The pressure on the hospital for beds was so great that they could keep me for only six days. Bill took me to his flat and moved furniture and beds so that he was within arms' reach at night. Four times a day he had to douche my feet in hot and cold water alternately and bandage them over a base of swathed cotton wool. His patience was limitless, and he served tea and cakes on his sunny balcony to my visitors while keeping a watchful eye at all times on my hesitant steps on crutches. He was nurse, comforter and the source of new strength.

Eventually we decided to live together. He has his own bedroom and his old single bed. But we bought for my room a king-sized, five-foot-wide divan bed with a blue velvet headboard. When the spirit moves us we go to bed early and lie close to each other and laugh and talk about everything and anything as long as it's not serious. Problems are barred.

We do most things together, but as we have both been used to a high degree of independence we need to separate sometimes. I play golf at my club and Bill attends a photographic club. We both have family, although, sadly, neither of us are in close touch with our relatives. The contact is minimal. In real terms we have only each other, but we feel that God is never far away. For Bill's eightieth birthday we have booked a weekend in Paris.

Commentary

This account is reprinted with permission from the report of the

National Conference of Age Concern England that was held from 24 to 25 July 1989.

Several things are not quite clear in this account. The narrator tells us that he spent a quarter of a century as a widower, so presumably he has been married but never remarried. Whether during this period he had any heterosexual or homosexual passing relationships is left unclear. It is not so very unusual for men to be bisexual in orientation, but it is probably less usual for men who have previously been married to settle for a stable homosexual relationship in later life. This man notes that both Bill and he are accustomed to a 'high degree of independence', and it is possible that living with another man, rather than a woman, partly results from this. It may also be noted that although this couple like going to bed together, which may involve some erotic contact, whatever they talk about, 'problems are barred'. This implies a somewhat stringent limitation on their psychological closeness, a lack of intimacy that would not generally be found in heterosexual couples.

Homosexual relationships are as varied as heterosexual ones: some individuals with a very solitary and introverted nature may feel uncomfortable getting too emotionally close to anyone else. As women, in general, are more likely to expect quite a close emotional relationship with a lover they are living with, an introverted man may feel more at ease with another man. This couple give one another companionship, physical tenderness – as in Bill's gentle nursing after his friend came out of hospital – and presumably erotic satisfaction in the king-sized bed they bought together.

We are told that both have families, but it is not clear what these families consist of. Do the two men have children? If so then both have been involved in a heterosexual relationship in the past. For reasons that are not stated they are now out of touch with their families. This sort of relationship is discussed in

Raymond Berger's book *Gay and Gray: The Older Homosexual Man*. Some men in this sort of later-life relationship have had very unhappy experiences in their sexual relationships with women in the past and have settled for partnerships in which they feel safer. Berger comments, 'Having completed this study I feel more disturbed than ever about the fact that almost every gerontological researcher and commentator has chosen to ignore older folk who happen to be homosexual. Can these researchers believe that homosexuals self-destruct at the age of forty? Or have they simply been unaware of the millions of older people who are homosexual?'

I think the matter is complex and we should not make the mistake of dividing people into heterosexuals and homosexuals as though they were two different species. Society now tolerates a wide range of different expressions of love and eroticism at all ages. The particular form that an individual opts for may depend not only on some innate disposition but on the particular relationships that he or she has experienced during the course of a lifetime.

Notes

Introduction

1. H. B. Gibson, *The Emotional and Sexual Lives of Older People: A Manual for Professionals*, London: Chapman and Hall, 1992.
2. A. C. Kinsey, W. B. Pomeroy and C. E. Martin, *Sexual Behavior in the Human Male*, Philadelphia: W. B. Saunders, 1948. See also A. C. Kinsey, W. B. Pomeroy, C. E. Martin and P. H. Gebhard, *Sexual Behavior in the Human Female*, Philadelphia: W. B. Saunders, 1953.
3. Wendy Greengross and Sally Greengross, *Living, Loving and Ageing*, Mitcham: Age Concern, 1989, p. 93.
4. Betty Friedan, *The Fountain of Age*, London: Jonathan Cape, 1994.

1. What is love?

1. Isaac Bashevis Singer, *Old Love*, Harmondsworth: Penguin Books, 1982.
2. Margaret Mead, cited in John A. Lee, *Lovestyles*, London: Abacus, 1976, p. 1.
3. William Shakespeare, 'Sonnet 116', in *The Works of William Shakespeare*, London: Basil Blackwell, 1947.
4. Algernon Swinburne, 'Hymn to Proserpine', in *Swinburne: Selected Poems*, L. M. Finday (ed.), Manchester: Fyfied Books, 1982.
5. Georges Bizet, *Carmen*, London: Pagoda, 1987.
6. Lord Byron, *Don Juan*, London: Phoenix, 1996.
7. William Blake, 'The Clod and the Pebble', in Geoffrey Keynes (ed.), *Poetry and Prose of William Blake*, London: Nonsuch Press, 1927.
8. Plato, *The Republic*, tr. H. D. P. Lee, Harmondsworth: Penguin Books, 1955.

9. C. S. Lewis, *The Four Loves*, London: Geoffrey Bles, 1960.

10. John Carey, 'Oxford's Beer and Baccy Brigade', in *Original Copy*, London: Faber and Faber, 1987.

11. *Shorter Oxford English Dictionary*, 3rd edn, vol. 1, Oxford: Oxford University Press, 1964.

12. Rollo May, *Love and Will*, London: Souvenir Press, 1970.

13. John A. Lee, *Lovestyles*, London: J. M. Dent and Sons, 1976.

14. *Ibid.*, p. 6.

15. *Ibid.*, pp. 13–14.

16. William Preston cited in Lee, *Lovestyles*.

17. I refer to the bowdlerized version published by Robert Burns. The original version, which was published in *The Merry Muses* after Burns's death, was quite bawdy and will be referred to later.

18. Lee's *Lovestyles* was originally published in Canada in 1973 under the title *Colours of Love: An Exploration of the Ways of Loving*: New Press.

19. Nancy Daton and Dean Roheaver, 'Beyond Generativity: Towards a Sensuality of Later Life', in R. B. Weg (ed.), *Sexuality in the Later Years*, New York and London: Academic Press, 1983.

2. Late love in literature

1. Aristophanes, 'Ecclesiazusae', in *The Comedies of Aristophanes*, vol. 2, tr. W. S. Hickey, London: G. Bell and Sons, 1885.

2. Quoted by W. Barnstone, *Greek Lyric Poetry*, New York: Bantam Books, 1967.

3. John Donne, 'Elegies: The Autumnal', in *Love Poems*, London: Phoenix, 1996.

4. Plato, *The Republic*, p. 53.

5. Geoffrey Chaucer, 'Merchant's Tale', *The Canterbury Tales*, tr. David Wright, London: Fontana, 1964.

6. Chaucer, 'Prologue to the Wife of Bath's Tale', *The Canterbury Tales*.

7. William Shakespeare, 'The Passionate Pilgrim', in *The Works of William Shakespeare*.

8. Don Charles, 'Literary Old Age: A Browse Through History',

Educational Gerontology, vol. 2, 1977, pp. 237–53.

9. Saul Bellow, *Mr Sammler's Planet,* London: Viking Press, 1970.

10. Mary Sohngen, 'The Experience of Old Age as Depicted in Contemporary Novels', *The Gerontologist,* vol. 17, 1977, pp. 70–78.

11. Sawako Ariyoshi, *The Twilight Years,* tr. Mildred Tarahara, London: Peter Owen, 1984.

12. Junichiro Tanizaki, *Diary of a Mad Old Man,* tr. Howard Hibbert, New York: Alfred A. Knopf, 1965.

13. D. Fisher, *Growing Old in America,* Oxford: Oxford University Press, 1977.

14. Graham Greene, *Travels With My Aunt,* Geneva: Heron Books, 1982.

15. Muriel Spark, *Memento Mori,* London: Macmillan, 1959.

16. John Donne, 'Ecstasie', in *The Love Poems of John Donne,* London: Chatto and Windus, 1937.

17. Kingsley Amis, *Ending Up,* Harmondsworth: Penguin Books, 1974.

18. Kingsley Amis, *The Old Devils,* London: Century, 1986.

19. Eudora Welty, 'Old Mr Marblehall', in *The Collected Stories of Eudora Welty,* Harmondsworth: Penguin Books, 1983.

20. V. S. Pritchett, 'The Spree', in *The Camberwell Beauty,* London: Random House, 1974.

21. Robert Burns, 'John Anderson My Jo', in *The Poetical Works of Robert Burns,* London: Senate, 1994.

22. J. Barke and S. Goodsir Smith (eds.), *The Merry Muses of Caledonia,* Edinburgh: McDonald, 1992.

23. James Kinsey, cited in Alan Bold, *A Burns Companion,* London: Macmillan, 1991.

24. Dylan Thomas, *The Dylan Thomas Omnibus,* London: Phoenix, 1995.

25. Bernard Malamud, 'In Retirement', *Rembrandt's Hat,* New York: Farrar, Straus and Giroux, 1973.

26. John Cheever, *The World of Apples,* New York: Knopf, 1973.

27. Celeste Loughman, 'Eros and the Elderly: A Literary Review', *The Gerontologist,* vol. 20, 1983, pp. 182–7.

28. Louis de Bernières, *Captain Corelli's Mandolin,* London: Minerva, p. 424.

29. Gabriel García Márquez, *Love in the Time of Cholera*, tr. Edith Grossman, London: Cape, 1988, p. 339.
30. William Shakespeare, 'Sonnet 116'.

3. Popular media images

1. J. Lambert, P. Laslett and H. Clay, *The Image of the Elderly on TV*, Cambridge: University of the Third Age in Cambridge, 1984.
2. Lambert, Laslett and Clay, *Image of the Elderly*, Section 7.
3. Lambert, Laslett and Clay, *Image of the Elderly*, Section 8.
4. Eric Midwinter, *Out of Focus: Old Age, the Press and Broadcasting*, London: Centre for Policy on Ageing, 1991.
5. Midwinter, *Out of Focus*, pp. 15–16.
6. *Mail on Sunday*, 23 February 1991, pp. 24–5.
7. Quoted by Midwinter, *Out of Focus*, p. 47.
8. Cited in E. Cumming and W. Henry, *Growing Old: The Process of Disengagement*, New York: Basic Books, 1961.
9. Cited in John Richman, 'The Foolishness and Wisdom of Age: Attitudes Toward the Elderly as Reflected in Jokes', *The Gerontologist*, vol. 1, 1977, pp. 210–19.
10. Christopher Watson, *Jokes: Form, Content, Use and Function*, London: Academic Press, 1979.
11. Cited in Richman, 'The Foolishness and Wisdom of Age', pp. 210–19.

4. New partnerships

1. Greengross and Greengross, *Living, Loving and Ageing*.
2. E. B. Palmore, 'The Prediction of Longevity Differences', *The Gerontologist*, vol. 22, 1982, pp. 513–18.
3. Margaret Mead, 'Marriage in Two Steps', *Redbook*, July, 1966.
4. William Shakespeare, 'Hamlet', in *The Works of William Shakespeare*.
5. Robert N. Butler, and Myrna I. Lewis, *Love and Sex After Sixty*, New York: Harper and Row, 1988, p. 140.

6. Alex Comfort, *The Joy of Sex* (revised), London: Quartet Books, 1987.
7. See Further Reading.
8. B. D. Starr and M. B. Weiner, *The Starr-Weiner Report on Sex and Sexuality in the Mature Years*, New York: McGraw Hill, 1981.
9. Jill Pitkeathley and David Emerson, *Age Gap Relationships*, London: Thorsons, 1995.
10. *Ibid.*, p. 111.
11. *Ibid.*, p. 32.
12. *Ibid.*, p. 43.
13. *Ibid.*, p. 121.

5. Four late marriages

1. Bertrand Russell, *Marriage and Morals*, London: Allen and Unwin, 1929.
2. Bertrand Russell, *The Autobiography of Bertrand Russell*, vol. 1, London: Allen and Unwin, 1967, p. 13.
3. Caroline Moorhead, *Bertrand Russell: A Life*, London: Sinclair-Stevenson, 1992, p. 59.
4. *Ibid.*, p. 61.
5. Russell, *Autobiography of Bertrand Russell*, pp. 147–8.
6. *Ibid.*, p. 146.
7. Moorhead, *Bertrand Russell*, p. 59.
8. Russell, *Autobiography of Bertrand Russell*, p. 205.
9. Dora Russell, *The Tamarisk Tree*, Vol. 1, London: Clerk/Pemberton, 1975, p. 248.
10. Cited in Russell, *Tamarisk Tree*, p. 222.
11. Moorhead, *Bertrand Russell*, p. 543.
12. Katharine Tait, *My Father Bertrand Russell*, London: Victor Gollancz, 1976, p. 178.
13. David Robinson, *Chaplin: His Life and Art*, London: Collins, 1985.
14. Charles Chaplin, *My Autobiography*, London: Bodley Head, 1964, p. 328.
15. *Ibid.*, pp. 420–21.

16. Charles Chaplin Jnr, *My Father Charlie Chaplin*, cited in Robinson, *Chaplin: His Life and Art*.

17. *Daily Herald*, 16 April 1959.

18. *Ibid.*

19. Kathleen Adams, *George Eliot: A Brief Biography*, Warwick: Warwick County Council, 1976.

20. Gordon S. Haight, *George Eliot: A Biography*, London: Oxford University Press, 1968, p. 49.

21. Gordon S. Haight, *George Eliot and John Cross with Chapman's Diaries*, London: Oxford University Press, 1940, p. 50.

22. Haight, *George Eliot: A Biography*, p. 56.

23. Haight, *George Eliot and John Cross*.

24. Gordon S. Haight, *Selections from George Eliot's Letters*, New Haven: Yale University Press, 1954.

25. Haight, *George Eliot: A Biography*, p. 964.

26. Eliza L. Linton, *The Bookman*, Vol. 3, 1893, p. 52.

27. John W. Cross, *George Eliot's Life as Related in Her Letters and Journals*, Leipzig: Tauchnitz, 1885.

28. Maurice Goudeket, *Close to Colette*, tr. Enid McLeod, London: Secker and Warburg, 1957.

29. Cited in Yvonne Mitchell, *Colette: A Taste for Life*, London: Weidenfeld and Nicolson, 1975, p. 72.

30. *Ibid.*, p. 81.

31. *Ibid.*, p. 113.

32. Bertrand de Jouvenel, *Un Voyageur dans le siècle*, Paris: Laffont, 1979.

33. Reynaud de Juvenel, cited in Mitchell, *Colette: A Taste for Life*.

34. Herbert Lottman, *Colette: A Life*, London: Minerva, 1992.

6. *Staying together*

1. Robert Browning, 'Rabbi ben Ezra', *The Poetical Works of Robert Browning*, London: Smith, Elder and Co., 1902.

2. W. B. Yeats, 'When You Are Old' in *The Collected Poems of*

W. B. Yeats, London: Macmillan, 1933.

4. Starr and Weiner, *The Starr-Weiner Report*.

5. Edward M. Brecher, *Love, Sex and Aging*, Boston: Little, Brown and Co., 1984.

6. *Ibid.*, p. 57.

7. *Ibid.*, p. 58.

8. Age Concern England. *Proceedings of the Annual National Conference of Age Concern England*, Mitcham: Age Concern England, 1989.

9. Greengross and Greengross, *Living, Loving and Ageing*.

10. Alex Comfort, *A Good Age*, London: Pan Books, 1990.
    R. N. Butler and M. I. Lewis, *Love and Sex After Sixty*. New York: Harper and Row, 1988.

11. E. Pfeiffer, A. Verwoerdt and G. C. Davis, 'Sexual Behavior in Middle Life', *American Journal of Psychiatry*, vol. 128, 1972, pp. 1264–8.

12. *Ibid.*, p. 117.

13. *Ibid.*, p. 118.

Further reading

ROBERT N. BUTLER AND MYRNA I. LEWIS (1988) *Love and Sex After Sixty*. New York: Harper and Row

R. BERGER (1980) *Gay and Gray: The Older Homosexual Man*. Urbana: University of Illinois Press

EDWARD M. BRECHER (1984) *Love , Sex and Aging: A Consumer Union Report*. Boston: Little Brown and Co.

ALEX COMFORT (1990) *A Good Age*. London: Pan Books

H. B. GIBSON (1992) *The Emotional and Sexual Lives of Older People*. London: Chapman and Hall

H. B. GIBSON (1997) *A Little of What You Fancy Does You Good: Your Health in Later Life*. London: Third Age Press

WENDY AND SALLY GREENGROSS (1988) *Living, Loving and Ageing: Sexual and Personal Relationships in Later Life*. London: Age Concern England

JOHN A. LEE (1976) *Lovestyles*. London: J. M. Dent and Sons

JILL PITKEATHLEY AND DAVID EMERSON (1995) *Age Gap Relationships*. London: Thorsons

Third Age News (published quarterly by the Third Age Trust, 26 Harrison Street, London WC1H 8JG). This gives details of the University of the Third Age, which has over three hundred local branches in the UK and a membership in excess of 50,000. Its primary aim is to provide low-cost educational and social opportunities to people in later life who are no longer in full-time employment. There are no entrance qualifications and the branches are autonomous, depending on the self-help principle, without the aid of paid tutors.